The Journey from JACOB to Israel

Other Biblical Character Studies by Walter C. Kaiser, Jr.

The Lives and Ministries of ELIJAH and ELISHA

ABRAHAM The Friend of God

JOSHUA A True Servant Leader

The Journey from JACOB to Israel

Coming Soon

DAVID A Man After God's Own Heart

MOSES The Man Who Saw the Invisible God

JOSEPH From Prison to Palace

NEHEMIAH The Wall Builder

SOLOMON The King with a Listening Heart

THE TWELVE The "Minor" Prophets Speak Today

ZECHARIAH The Quintessence of Old Testament Prophecy

DANIEL The Handwriting is on the Wall

RUTH The Moabite and the Providence of God

ESTHER God Preserves the Jewish Nation

The Journey from JACOB to Israel

Walter C. Kaiser, Jr.

Lederer Books
an imprint of
Messianic Jewish Publishers
Clarksville, MD 21029

Unless otherwise noted, all Scripture quotations are from the *New American Standard Bible*, copyright © 1978 by Thomas Nelson Publishers; the *Complete Jewish Bible*, copyright © 1998 by Messianic Jewish Publishers; or the *New International Version*, copyright © 2002 by the International Bible Society.

Printed in the United States of America

Cover Design by Lisa Rubin,
Messianic Jewish Publishers
Graphic Design by Yvonne Vermillion,
Magic Graphix.com
Editor, George August Koch

1 2021
ISBN 978-1-951833-17-6

Published by
Lederer Books
An imprint of Messianic Jewish Publishers
6120 Day Long Lane
Clarksville, MD 21029

Distributed by
Messianic Jewish Publishers & Resources
Order line: (800) 410-7367
lederer@messianicjewish.net
www.MessianicJewish.net

For all those who earnestly desire
to walk with our Lord…
— 1 Corinthians 2:9

Table of Contents

Introduction

Jacob: Deceiver, Now "Striver with God"

Genesis 25:19–35:29

Jacob is the original ancestor of the nation of Israel by virtue of being the father of all the 12 tribes of Israel (25:1ff). He was the son of Isaac and Rebekah and younger twin to his brother Esau, and later became the husband of Leah and Rachel (25:21–26, 29:21–30). Jacob's name at first built on the Hebrew word for "heel," meaning "the one who grasps the heel" of his brother as he came out of his mother's womb. But his name also could be rendered "he who cheats, supplants" (25:26; 27:30), for he was a real schemer. Later, God changed his name to "Israel" (32:28; 49:2).

Even though Jacob's faith shines through the Genesis narratives, his life is a narrative of conflict, one in which he always seemed to be running from someone or something—such as from his brother Esau, his mother's brother Laban, or the famine in Canaan. His life was peppered with rebellion, and every time he escaped one trial, he found himself facing another!

Four New Testament passages recall aspects of his life. There's the episode of the woman at the well in Sychar, which Yeshua declared was provided for all by the patriarch Jacob (John 4:12). Stephen mentioned Jacob's name as this newly named deacon stood before the Sanhedrin in defense of his actions (Acts 7:8–16). In another instance, the Apostle Paul used Jacob as an example of God's sovereign choice and predestination of the elect (Romans 9:10–13). And the author of Hebrews used Jacob as an example of what real, active faith was all about (Hebrews 11:9, 20–22).

A Short Outline of the Life of Jacob

If the story of Jacob's son Joseph is included in the total count, then Jacob's story covers something like one-half of the book of Genesis. Jacob is first presented in Genesis as living up to his name of "deceiver" or "cheater" by bargaining for his brother Esau's birthright. Moreover, a household that included parental partiality was responsible for a long line of hostility wherein Esau, the hunter, was favored by his father Isaac, while Jacob, the more reclusive, quiet homebody, and settled son, was favored by his mother Rebekah. So strong were the tensions between the twins that at times it seemed this rift threatened the very fulfillment of the promise-plan of God itself.

Esau recklessly gave up his birthright to Jacob, which uninformed Isaac tried to bestow in his blessing on his favored son Esau. But the word that Rebekah received (25:23) seemed to encourage her to counter Isaac's will and see to it that the blessing actually came to Jacob, *her* favorite son. It all ended up with the blind father Isaac pronouncing the blessing he had intended for Esau over Jacob's head. Isaac did give a lesser blessing to Esau, but he was destined to serve Jacob and live in the less-fertile land of Edom (27:40).

The rift between the twins was so severe that Rebekah had to arrange for Jacob to flee back to her home in Paddan-Aram to escape Esau's wrath (27:41–28:5). Thus, at 40 years of age, Jacob fled from his home in Canaan. As he journeyed to his mother's homestead, one night at Bethel his attention was arrested by a vision of the Lord showing him his responsibilities as the heir of the promises God had made to Abraham (28:10–22).

When he arrived at his mother's relatives an-Ain Paddram, Jacob the "deceiver" met up with Laban, who likewise was a trickster and tricked him into marrying Leah, Laban's elder daughter, before Jacob could marry Rachel, the younger daughter, whom he had bargained for and expected to marry. In total, Jacob served 14 years for his two wives (29:1–30) and six more years to gain the wealth he was able to accrue at Laban's expense. Even after Laban relentlessly changed Jacob's wages ten times (31:7, 41), God still prospered Jacob in astounding ways. Each wife of Jacob was given a maidservant by Laban, so that from the four women he eventually had a family of 12 children (29:31–30:24).

Jacob left Aram/Syria after twenty years of service to Laban, supported by his wives who also claimed they too had been cheated out of their dowry (31:15). While Laban and his sons were away from home shearing sheep, Jacob, and all he had, got a three-day advantage on escaping from Laban, but were overtaken when they reached Gilead, having already traveled some 400 miles from Haran.

Laban complained that Jacob had not allowed him an opportunity to say goodbye to his daughters and offer the appropriate feast. But even more importantly, he wanted to discover who it was who had stolen his gods (31:30, 32), for somehow whoever owned these gods also had the inheritance-will in their hands! These idols were not found among any of the possessions of any of Jacob's entourage, but the text tells us that it was Rachel who had absconded with Laban's will.

Laban suggested a covenant of friendship that would include these terms: (1) Jacob would not ill-treat his wives, (2) Jacob would not marry any other women, and (3) together the two men would establish the place where the covenant had been concluded as the boundary neither one of the two men would ever cross over with evil intent!

As Jacob approached the land the Lord had promised him, he was met by a host of angels at Mahanaim (32:1–2). No doubt they were agents of God's protection as Jacob got closer and closer to meeting his brother Esau, who he had not seen for 20 years! To ward off any possible danger and lingering hostility from Esau, Jacob wisely sent a most-elaborate gift ahead of his entourage to ease the way for this meeting with his brother. Jacob divided his group into two segments, each large enough to defend themselves should it be necessary and prayed to God for safety.

After his contingents had crossed the Jabbok River, Jacob met One who wrestled with him all night until daybreak (32:24). This match continued into the early morning without either one gaining the upper hand. Jacob refused to let his antagonist go until that One blessed him. That blessing would only come after Jacob answered the man's question, "What is your name?" Jacob was renamed Israel, meaning "he who strives with God" or "God strives." That place was named Peniel ("face of God"), for Jacob had seen God face-to-face and been spared (32:30).

When the two brothers finally met, Esau seemed to be satisfied to forget the old conflicts that had separated them. Esau headed south to Seir and became the father of the Edomites. The two men never met again until their father's death (35:27–29). Jacob, however, traveled from Succoth to Shechem, where he built an altar to the Lord. At Shechem, the son of Hamor, the city ruler, raped Jacob's daughter Dinah. Later, when Jacob's sons returned, they demanded the Shechemites be circumcised before an intermarriage of their sister could be consummated with Hamor's son. However, this was a deception, and when the complying men of Shechem were recovering from their surgeries and unable to defend themselves, Simeon and Levi avenged their sister by killing all the men of that tribe.

Jacob went on from Shechem to Bethel where the promises of God were repeated to him. There Deborah, his mother's nurse, died (35:8), and Rachel died while giving birth to Benjamin at Ephrath

(35:19, 48:7). Reuben, Jacob's firstborn son, forfeited his honor of being the eldest son by sexual misconduct with his father's concubine Bilhah (35:22). As the story ended, Isaac, who had been robbed of the companionship of both of his sons, finally brought the two boys together as the family buried him at Hebron in the family cave of Macpelah.

When another famine hit the land, Jacob went with his sons to Egypt, and he dwelt in that foreign land at the site of Goshen until his death. He too was finally laid to rest in Hebron at the cave Abraham had purchased (50:12, 14).

Lesson 1

Jacob Steals His Brother Esau's Birthright

Genesis 25:19–34

With the appearance of the rubric "This is the account of the family line of Abraham's son Isaac" (25:19), we have reached the midpoint of Genesis and another major section in the book. From here on out, the life of one of the twins born to Isaac and Rebekah, Abraham's grandson Jacob, will occupy our focus. From how things were presented, it may have seemed we would now be introduced to a narrative about Isaac; but instead, it is mostly about the sons of Isaac—Esau and Jacob. However, in many ways, the character and personalities of Jacob and Abraham will offer us a good number of contrasts in chapters 25–36. Only in chapter 26 will the narrative be about Isaac.

Still, we will see there are numerous similarities between the Isaac stories and the other patriarchal narratives. The problem of barrenness seems to be found all through the narratives; Sarah, Rebekah, Rachel (29:31), and Leah (29:35) are similarly afflicted. It is clear that if that part of the promise-plan of God—who promised a "seed" through this chosen seed—is to be accomplished, it certainly will not happen because of the attention given it by these families in their human efforts, but only because of God's wonderful intervention.

Isaac's Wife Rebekah Bears Twins – Genesis 25:19–28

Again, the story of a new patriarch begins with the problem of barrenness. In the case of Abraham and Sarah, the matter was spread over multiple chapters in Genesis, with a mountain of challenges to their faith. However, in the case of the Isaac and Rebekah story, the whole episode of barrenness was reduced to one verse—*Isaac prayed to Adonai on behalf of his wife because she was childless. Adonai heeded his prayer and Rebecca became pregnant* (v. 25:21).

Abraham and Sarah became the father and mother of Isaac. He was 40 years old when he married Rebekah, the daughter of Bethuel, the Aramean from Paddan-Aram and sister of Laban, also an Aramean (vv. 19–20). Moreover, Isaac prayed about his wife's barren condition, but the text gives the impression that Isaac's faith was so in tune with God that he received a rather immediate positive answer from the Lord (v. 21). Surely there was no prolonged delay, as seemed to be the case with Sarah, for the text simply records that Isaac prayed and the Lord answered directly.

Rebekah's complaint was of a much different nature—that the babies were "jostling" each other in her womb (v. 22). She was so perplexed over the seriousness of this unusual prenatal condition that she went to the Lord and asked why this was happening in her womb! (v. 22b) Now the twins had been born twenty years after Isaac and Rebekah's wedding (v. 26), but what was the meaning of this internal struggle in the womb? Was this an event permitted by the Lord to be something to match Abraham and Sarah's years of waiting during her barrenness? Or was this a warning that what had begun in the womb would continue long after the twins were born? They continued to "thrash against each other with their *feet*," for their agitation against each other was so vigorous that Rebekah feared they would crush one another.

In the Lord's communication to Rebekah, he alerts her, "Two nations are in your womb, and two peoples from within you will be separated; one people will be stronger than the other, and the older will serve the younger" (v. 23). This would become a central theme for the remaining narrative in Genesis. The struggle between the brothers that had begun in Rebekah's womb is reminiscent of the struggle between Cain and Abel in Genesis 4. But that same type of struggle seemed to have been replicated in the conflict that erupted between the sons of Noah (9:20–27), as it was also manifested between Abraham and Lot (13:7–12), Isaac and Ishmael (21:9), Jacob and Laban (chapters 29–31), and the conflict between Joseph and his brothers (chapters 37–50). That's a lot of conflict!

This thrashing in Rebekah's womb seems to set the stage for Jacob's hand and Esau's heel to both be involved at their birth, especially with the thrashing about and flailing of the boy's *feet* (25:26)!

At any rate, God announces a destiny for the two nations that were in Rebekah's womb. This raised the question as to whether the destiny of these two nations is foreordained by God. Should we regard this struggle in the womb as one that God has permitted between them that would impact their futures as being a life in which we would have one brother set off against the other one? Should this contest between the boys be seen as a struggle, not only of fetal vigor, but also as one of inherited drives and a love for conflict that would endure in life?

Laban, the twins' uncle, has already been seen as very aggressive and constantly on the lookout for whatever economic advantage he could gain (note, for example, how he reacted when he saw Sarah's jewelry). But if there might be the source for some of that same aggressiveness on the part of Jacob that was in the genes of the family, then that might be where Esau got his drive from—such as an earlier ancestor like Laban. No doubt Esau preferred hunting animals on the open range, rather then herding the flock and dwelling in tents, as Jacob enjoyed (25:27). Is our Lord, then, announcing his "election" here, or is he indicating which of the two will prevail?

The two boys are not named casually; Jacob receives his name by holding his firstborn twin's heel. Was this an indication that he was unwilling to stop the fetal wrestling, even for a short spell? Esau, on the other hand, is named for the mantle of hair that covers his body. (Should his English name then be "Harry"?) Later, Esau is called Edom, because of the pottage that is red (Hebrew *'edom*) just as he was at birth! These men may be twins, but they are by no means identical or even similar in most ways. Moreover, Esau loved to hunt wild game in the field, and Isaac, his father, loved Esau for his meat. On the other hand, Jacob was not a "quiet man" as the NIV puts it, but he was a tent-dweller, a veritable "home-body, characterized by the Hebrew word *tam*, whose English meaning is unclear. Some render this word as "plain," others as "quiet," but it must be the opposite of the man of the field! Jacob was favored and loved by Rebekah, but why? Was her love kindled by the annunciation given to her, or was it because Isaac held Jacob in lower regard? Whatever the case, this division of parental regard surely only intensified the conflict between the boys, if not also between the parents.

Some try to get at the difference between the two men as a parallel to the story in *The Epic of Gilgamesh*, about the legendary king of Uruk in Babylonia. In this story, the man of the steppe named Enkidu is a man much like Esau, who was covered with hair all over his body, so that he was hardly distinguishable from the animals. But a courtesan, who seemed to be cast in a different way, was the other son Jacob; he was a *tam*.

To continue our Mesopotamian story, word was sent after just seven days from the city of Uruk to lure Enkidu to that city to meet Gilgamesh. Immediately the difference between Enkidu and the animals becomes clear. Furthermore, when Enkidu begins to anoint his body with oil and puts on clothing as preparation to go into the city, it seems he becomes more human.

Some use this Mesopotamian story to show the difference between Esau and Jacob. In the view of some, Esau is the "natural" man, a sort of "lone ranger," who lives by hunting and one who loves the taste of wild meat. Jacob, however, is not like that natural man who loves the hunt, but he is one having *tam*—not meaning one who has "integrity," but a word from the more-likely cognate Hebrew verb *tamam*, which would point to "completion"—one who was capable of moral and spiritual relations. At any rate, the two men were really different!

Esau Sells His Birthright to Jacob for Some Red Stew – 25:29–34

Because Jacob seemed to spend a lot of time at home, he must have learned to become a good cook. Thus, it happened that one day as Jacob had just finished making a pot of red-lentil stew, Esau dragged himself into the tent, exhausted from the day's hunt out in the open fields. Famished and really exhausted, Esau begged Jacob for a portion of his reddish stew. Perhaps it was this incident that gave Esau the nickname of "red" (v. 30); but it is also true that when he had emerged from his mother's womb, he was "red" (v. 25). So, for one reason or the other—or perhaps because of both situations—the nickname "red" stuck.

Jacob agreed to give his brother some of the stew, but he cut a tough bargain with him—Esau would have to willing to trade his birthright for the stew! Jacob asked Esau to sell his birthright of being the firstborn in the family in exchange for some lentil stew! That birthright given to the firstborn would have been eventually worth Esau receiving twice as much of the inheritance from their father Isaac's estate at his death (Deuteronomy 21:17), but Esau was too hungry and exhausted to debate the issue, so he agreed to sell that birthright to his younger brother in exchange for the stew.

Such sales of birthrights are not unknown in the ancient Near East, for such a sale is exhibited in the Nuzi texts. But the point was this: Esau showed he despised his birthright (25:34). It is amazing, the writer of Hebrews 12:16 concludes, that Esau was willing to sell his own birthright in exchange for a single meal. And so went the life of Esau!

Conclusions

1. We have left the story of Abraham in Genesis 11–25:17, the man who was God's friend, and now we pick up the life of Abraham's grandson, Jacob. There are some pleasing similarities in the strong characteristics of both men, but Jacob also affords us a look at some basic contrasts as well.
2. The theme of barrenness once again arises in the marriage of Isaac and his wife Rebekah. From a human perspective, this hardly appears to be the way to fulfill the promise of numerous seed to the promise-couple by beginning with a state of barrenness.
3. When Rebekah does conceive, she has twins named Esau and Jacob—two boys who could not be more different from each other and who jostled each other even in the womb.
4. Parental favoritism wreaks a lot of havoc in this family as the parents' favor is split between the two sons.
5. Esau sells his birthright for a mess of lentil stew, showing his low regard for the gift of being the firstborn of the two sons.

Questions for Thought or Discussion

1. How would you contrast the characters of Jacob and Esau?
2. What do you make of the fact that the twin boys in Rebekah's womb jostled each other? How will that kind of struggle affect the way both men will live in the days to come?
3. Did God elect Jacob to be the one who would inherit his brother's birthright, or did he earn it as a reward for outmaneuvering his brother?
4. Why did God bless Isaac so bountifully that it prompted Abimelech to expel him from Philistia (26:12, 16)?

Lesson 2

The Life of Isaac, Jacob's Son

Genesis 26:1–35

The story of the patriarchs can also be told as a story of a series of separations. The first separation was of Abraham the Shemite, from the other nations; the second separation was of Abraham from his family member Lot; the third was the separation made between Abraham's son of promise and other progeny; and the fourth separation was between the two twins of Abraham's son Isaac—Esau and Jacob!

Isaac does not strike us as an especially exciting personality, for his achievements are often at best seen as lackluster, ordinary, bland, and passive, especially when compared to what his father Abraham was able to do. Some think the case for Isaac's significance is so poor that his only claim to fame is his longevity—he outlived his father by five years, living to the age of 180 (35:28). It is nevertheless true that Isaac experienced God's generous blessing and protection as he rose to a position of prominent wealth and respect. It is said that Isaac manifested an "elasticity of endurance"; according to some, he exuded a special greatness that has been transmitted as an "ineradicable tenaciousness" to the nation descended from him! Possibly!

The Renewal of the Promise at Gerar – 26:1–6

In the seven short histories in this chapter, we are given the independent story of Isaac covering his first forty years. Isaac didn't attain to his father Abraham's greatness; nevertheless, he did exemplify real endurance and was the recipient of an enormous amount of blessing and wealth from God. In some ways, Isaac's life was often a mere echo of his father's. But in other ways, he was a man of peace and a steady maintainer of all he had received from the Lord.

His narrative begins exactly as Abraham's story had: "Now there was a famine in the land." But in this case, Isaac did not descend into Egypt as his father and mother, Abraham and Sarah, had opted to, for the Lord appeared to him and commanded him not to go down into Egypt (26:2). Isaac, under divine instruction, was to remain in the land; therefore, he went to Gerar. No explanation is offered given why he must not go down to Egypt except the fact that he is to "live in the land" (v. 2).

Immediately following this directional note from the Lord, we are given the first reiteration of the Abrahamic Covenant, especially with the promise that the land is to be given to Isaac and his "offspring" (v. 3). Despite a pending famine, God promised he would be with Isaac, would bless him, and would ensure Isaac would indeed see all that had been promised to his father Abraham.

As the Lord had promised Abraham, so he now promises Isaac—his seed will be great in number as the stars in the sky (Gen. 12:2–4, 7); he would be given all the lands God had promised; and through his offspring, all the nations of the earth would be blessed.

What followed was rather remarkable, for in v. 5 the Lord noted that because Abraham had obeyed him, he had kept all his requirements (Hebrew *mishmarti*), commandments (*mitswotay*), decrees (*chuqqotay*), and laws (*wetorotay*), all of which are stated exactly in the same way in which obedience to the Sinaitic Covenant was later expressed (Deut. 11:1): "Love the LORD your God and keep his requirements, his decrees, his laws, and his commands." This wording resembles that of the Law of Moses. Perhaps this mystery is better resolved by noting how often Abraham had acted on several occasions in accordance with the law as found in Deuteronomy,[1] but there is no indication that he had an advanced written copy of the law. For example, when Abraham fought with the four kings from Mesopotamia, his actions closely paralleled what Deuteronomy 20 taught. In this 26th chapter of Genesis, the way Abraham treated the king of Sodom is much like what Deuteronomy 30:6 would instruct future leaders of defending Israel should act! Thus, the best solution to this so-called advance reading of the Law in this summary of Isaac's actions is to conclude that these may be early examples of the Law written instead on one's heart rather than written on stone or a parchment (as in Jeremiah 31:33).

This connection between the law and the heart seems to be reflected in Deuteronomy 30:11, 14, where Moses taught: "What I am commanding you [literally, 'this command'] is not too difficult for you or beyond your reach … it is in your mouth and in your heart so you may obey it." John Sailhamer concludes a noteworthy discussion of this text by pointing out how the Apostle Paul showed the same understanding of Deuteronomy 30 in Romans 10 where he too affirmed that the "words" of Moses that were "in your heart" were "the word of faith we are proclaiming" (Rom. 10:8).

God's Preservation of Isaac's Wife at Gerar – 26:7–11

In a way, one that was like Abraham's former habit of life, Isaac "stayed at Gerar" (20:1, 26:6). But even more significantly, as Abraham schemed with his wife by calling her his sister (12:13, 20:2), likewise Isaac pulls the same trick by calling his wife his "sister" (26:7). Therefore, just as Abraham needed to be rebuked by

---

1. This excellent discussion on law and faith is modeled after what John Sailhamer pointed to in Genesis: The Expositor's Bible Commentary, Vol. 1 (Grand Rapids: Zondervan, 2008), 229.

the Philistine king Abimelech for his shameful deed (20:9), so Isaac followed the same scheme and he too needed to be rebuked by Abimelech (26:10). No wonder the lives of these two biblical patriarchs are seen as following a similar course! There are, however, some key differences between these two men. In the episode of Abimelech and Sarah, it is most pointedly God who warned the pagan king not to touch Abraham's wife (20:6), but in the case of Isaac's wife Rebekah, Abimelech himself forbids anyone (including his own people) to touch or molest her (v. 11). Moreover, while it was God who said anyone who touched Sarah "will surely die" (20:7), in Rebekah's case it is Abimelech who threatens that anyone who molests Isaac's wife "shall surely be put to death" (v. 11).

Given so many similarities between the two stories, what is the author of Genesis trying to do? In chapter 20, the pagan king is said to be "pure of heart," or as the NIV has it, of "clear conscience," whereas in chapter 26 the pagan king has no need of being warned by God in a dream. Once Abimelech finds out who Rebekah is, he now regards his actions up to that point as ones that bring on him great shame (v. 10) or "guilt" (NIV).

So, what was the writer of Genesis trying to get at? The contrast between Isaac and Abimelech in chapter 26 shows the pagan king to be a pious and moral king in contrast to Isaac, who tried to cover up his wife's identity. To be sure, such a view of some of the neighboring nations to Abraham and Isaac were far and away different from the picture of what we found in the cities of Sodom and Gomorrah. There must have been pockets of those who followed God's general rule even if they did not put their full trust in him. Meanwhile, there were other pagans who were so far from heeding truth and righteousness that they were strictly for themselves as they mocked God and his righteousness.

The Blessing of God to Isaac Becomes Objectionable to King Abimelech – 26:12–17

The blessing of God continued even while Abraham and Isaac sojourned among the Gentiles. No wonder Isaac prospered so greatly with the crops he planted, the number of his flocks and herds, and the servants who worked for him, for 26:12 again tells us how God had blessed him.

We also see a new development in Isaac's history, for now he seems to unite agricultural sowing/planting and harvesting with the nomadic life of herding sheep and cattle—something that was not evident in the life of Abraham. This combination of occupations does not appear in full employment until we come to Israel's sojourn in Egypt, where we find the tillage of the land going on simultaneously together with raising cattle.

The wells Abraham's servants had dug (21:25–31) were stopped up and filled with earth and debris. This became a source of tension between Isaac and Abimelech—so much so, in fact, that Abimelech finally ordered Isaac to go away from him, for he had become too mighty for the Philistines (26:16). Therefore, Isaac left Abimelech and encamped in the Valley of Gerar and lived there.

The Restored and Newly Discovered Wells of Isaac – 26:18–22

The servants of Isaac dug wells in the valley and once again found a spring of living water (v. 19). Unfortunately, Abimelech's herdsmen fought with Isaac's herdsmen, contending that "the water belongs to us." Therefore, they called the spring Esek, meaning "contention" (v. 20). So, Isaac dug another well, which he named

Sitna, meaning "enmity." But contention rose between the rival herdsmen over that well too.

Patiently, Isaac abandoned claim to those two wells his men had dug previously. They then dug a third new well and named it Rehoboth, meaning "wide open spaces/room" (v. 22). The men of Abimelech did not contend with Isaac's men over this well, for Isaac concluded that God had made space/room for him so he could increase in the land.

Isaac Leaves Gerar and Moves to Beersheba – 26:23–25

Previously, after Abraham had separated from Lot, God gave Abraham a renewal of his promise of a land where he would live and enjoy great prosperity (13:14–17). Now, in like manner, the Lord spoke with Isaac as he returned to Beersheba (meaning "well of seven" or "well of the oath") by renewing his divine promise for a third time (26:23–24). The Lord promised once again to bless Isaac and multiply his descendants.

Isaac built an altar in Beersheba, where Abraham had lived for such a long time between his two sojourns in Hebron (18:1–19:23). Isaac stretched out his tent there, and his servants bored a well near his new living quarters. Beersheba was the place where two wells were dug and where two treaties with Abimelech had been made—the one made previously with Abraham, and another with Isaac.

King Abimelech Makes a Covenant with Isaac – 26:26–33

Here again we see another striking resemblance to the life of Abraham (v. 22). Suddenly Abimelech turned up at Isaac's place, accompanied by two men—Phicol, the commander of his forces, and Ahuzzath, his "friend" (a formal title, not a sign of friendship). Naturally, Isaac wanted to know, "Why have you come to me, since you were hostile to me and sent me away?" (v. 27)

Abimelech answered: "We [plainly] saw that the LORD was with you; so we said, 'There ought to be a sworn agreement between us'—between us and you. Let us make a treaty with you that you will do us no harm, just as we did not molest you, but always treated you well and sent you away in peace. And now you are blessed of the LORD" (vv. 28–29).

The blessing of God was more than a mere vacuous generalization, for even those in a Gentile nation could plainly see that the hand of the Lord was prospering Isaac, just as they had seen Abraham prosper under the same blessing.

The Marriages of Esau – 26:34–35

Esau, at 40 years of age, married two Hittite women. This is relatively insignificant for the story of the main line of the promise-plan of God, but these two verses serve as an important introduction to chapter 27. What is also striking is the name of Esau's first wife, Jehudith, which is a patronymic from the Hebrew word for "praise," similar to the tribal name "Judah." It is surprising to see this as an early Canaanite name.

Esau got married in the same 40th year that Isaac got married. Through all seven of the short stories in this 26th chapter, covering Isaac's first forty years, there is a continuous thread that shows how God blessed Isaac repeatedly as God's promise-plan continues to multiply. Even though Isaac's life constantly tends to echo Abraham's, he shows how he too was blessed repeatedly by the fame given to him by the Lord, who not only promised gifts to him but also fulfilled them.

Conclusions

1. Even though both Abraham's and Isaac's life begin with the presence of a famine, Isaac was definitely told not to go down to Egypt to avoid it. He was also told why he should not go there.
2. Isaac had learned an old trick from his father—to claim that Rebekah was his sister, which was not really true.
3. God continued to bless Isaac through his crops' productivity and his increase in his herds.
4. Isaac had loads of trouble over providing water for his herds, even though his men dug wells to water their flock. The men of Abimelech, the Philistine king, disputed the work they had initiated time after time.
5. Abimelech and his people could easily see how dramatically God was blessing Isaac in all he attempted.

Questions for Thought or Discussion

1. Does the character of Isaac stand out as forcefully as the character of Abraham? If not, why doesn't it?
2. Why did God tell Isaac not to go down to Egypt, but Abram did go to Egypt during a famine? Was there any sign of rebuke to Abram and Sarah?
3. What makes the women who came from Paddan-Aram so beautiful and so subject to being the possible basis for their husband's death?
4. To what degree can we find evidence of the law of God even before Moses wrote it? What was the source of these laws and terminology?
5. What evidence do you see in this text that Isaac worshiped the Lord?

Lesson 3

Jacob Steals the Birthright and Blessing from Esau

Genesis 27:1–40

Chapter 27 goes to quite a bit of detail to relate the story of Jacob's stealing of the birthright, for it is loaded with all its Near Eastern pageantry and suspense. However, despite the host of details, this narrative does not lose sight of the central theme of God's promise-plan. Isaac, who was one of those who was outmaneuvered in this story, correctly says: "I blessed him [Jacob]—and indeed he will be blessed" (v. 33).

Isaac, the Aged Father, Makes Preparation for Blessing His Oldest Son Esau – 27:1–4

There is a load of suspense in the way this story is told. An exhausted Esau, fresh from hunting game, had earlier sold his "birthright" (Hebrew *bekorah*) to Jacob for a pot of red-lentil soup. But now Jacob will wrest away from both his father and his brother the "blessing" (*berakhah*) Isaac was preparing to confer upon his eldest son Esau. But somehow, it seems, Jacob and Rebekah understood that Jacob needed both the "birthright" and the "blessing" to continue the plan promised by God.

This event falls in a time when Isaac has just passed his 100th birthday and his twin-sons their 40th birthdays (see 25:26, 26:34). As this story began, Isaac is depicted as "old and his eyes were so weak that he could no longer see" (v. 1). Then it was that Isaac called for his favored and eldest son Esau to come to him, for he felt it was time he gave his firstborn son his blessing. When Esau arrived, Isaac greeted him: "My son." Esau responded, "Here I am."

Then Isaac began by telling his son, "I am now an old man and [I] don't know the day of my death" (v. 2). So, this is what Isaac wanted his eldest son to do: "Now then, get your weapons—your quiver and bow—and go out to the open country to hunt some wild game for me. Prepare me the kind of tasty food I like and bring it to me to eat, so that I may give you a blessing before I die" (vv. 3–4).

So, Esau got his usual hunting equipment, a "quiver" and "shoulder belt" (see Isaiah 7:24). Isaac had a special taste for wild venison or the like, and this formed one of the strong attachments between father and this eldest son. Isaac, of course, could have blessed his son right then and there, but in God's providence, perhaps he wanted a sign of the willing obedience and a demonstration of Esau's affection for his father. But what Isaac did not know was this: "Now Rebekah was listening as Isaac spoke to his son Esau" (v. 5a). That would change everything—including the future!

Jacob's Mother Urges Jacob to Take to Isaac a Substitute Dish to Get His Father's Blessing – 27:5–10

Jacob and Rebekah conspired to prepare a spurious dish, like the wild animal meat Isaac loved, as Esau went off into the open fields to hunt his father's favorite game. Rebekah told her favorite son Jacob what she had overheard his father say to Esau. Rebekah must have been anticipating the day when her husband would show his hand by favoring their eldest son with the blessing and inheritance of the family, whereas she had the opposite point of view, for she had always wanted their youngest son to be the one who would be blessed and receive the inheritance (vv. 6–7).

After she had clued Jacob into what was going on, she laid out some very carefully conceived plans, which she may have been forming for some time. She told Jacob to go out to the flock and choose "two choice young goats" and she would prepare them just the way Isaac liked them fixed (vv. 8–9). Then she told Jacob to take this meal to his father to eat so he might give Jacob his blessing before he died (v. 10). The problem, however, was that to be effective, Isaac had to be deceived into thinking that the one who was offering the porridge was his eldest son Esau.

Rebekah Makes a Deceptive Garment for Jacob – 27:11–27

Jacob strongly protested his mother's plan. He pointed out that he had smooth skin, while Esau was hairy, and he was worried: "What if my father touches me? I would appear to be tricking him and it would bring down a curse on myself rather than a blessing" (v. 12). But Rebekah had an answer for that eventuality: Let the curse fall on her. With that settled, she dismissed Jacob with an order to go and get the two choice young goats so she could begin preparing Isaac's meal. Rebekah was so determined that Jacob be the one who was blessed, she was willing to incur the guilt herself. She was so willing to promote Jacob's receiving of this blessing that she was willing to do anything to promote its fulfillment. So, Jacob got the two young goats and brought them to his mother so she could prepare the food in a tasty and fitting manner; indeed, in the exact way that Isaac liked this dish prepared (v. 14).

Next, Rebekah located some of Esau's best clothes and put them on Jacob, and "covered his hands and the smooth part of his neck with the goatskins (vv. 15–16). After having finished all this preparation, she sent Jacob off with the morsels of food and the bread she had made (v. 17).

Isaac no longer could see, but he sensed something was wrong. He could not be sure what, but something just didn't seem to go together. When Jacob entered his presence, he approached his father and said, "My father" (v. 18a). Isaac replied, "Yes, my son, who is it?" (v. 18b) Jacob was already carrying out the plot his mother had hatched, so he answered his father's inquiry with a bald-faced lie: "I am Esau your firstborn. I have done as you told me. Please sit up and eat some game so that you may give me your blessing" (vv. 19–20). When Isaac asked how his son found the game so quickly, Jacob answered, "The LORD your God gave me success" (v. 20b)—he knew enough theology to give the right answers! Isaac still had his doubts, so he ordered the one who spoke to him, "Come near so I can touch you, my son, to know whether you are really my son Esau or not" (v. 21). This is exactly what Rebekah had anticipated when she covered Jacob with the goatskins! (We may wonder if she was in earshot while all of this was going on. The text does not say.)

One could imagine Jacob's heart beating wildly now, for he knew he had been lying. As Isaac touched him, he still could not make out what he should believe. He concluded: "The voice is the voice of Jacob, but the hands are the hands of Esau" (v. 22). Rebekah had accurately anticipated the tests her husband would use. Isaac, still not convinced, again asked Jacob: "Are you really my son Esau?" And once again Jacob lied, "I am" (v. 24).

With that quiz seemingly completed, Isaac asked his son to bring some of the game to eat, which Jacob did, and he also brought wine (v. 25). When Isaac had finished, he summoned his son to come to him and kiss him (v. 26), as if that were one final test. Jacob kissed his father, and as Esau's clothes were saturated with the odors of the vegetation of the field, this must have been the final convincing proof. Jacob had literally "passed the smell test." So, Isaac began to bless him (v. 27).

Isaac Unwittingly Blesses Jacob – 27:27a–29

Isaac began his blessing with the smell test of Esau's garments, which was still fresh in his nostrils: the smell of the fields the Lord had blessed (v. 27b). No doubt these fragrances reminded Isaac of the plains of the Promised Land. Moreover, God's promised blessing had brought the dew of heaven and the richness of the earth. This would mean an abundance of grain and new wine in plentiful portions. Thus, here is the beginning of the blessing of Abraham now passing to Isaac (Gen. 12:3, 7; 20:17), which he now bestows on his son in prophetic, poetic language. Furthermore, the blessing included the prayer that nations would serve this son of promise, peoples would bow down to him, and he would be lord over his brothers. What's more, those who would curse this son of promise would themselves be cursed, and those who would bless him would likewise be blessed (vv. 27b–29).

Many have pointed out the learned quotation of Genesis 27:29 by Balaam in Numbers 24:9b from this text as one that identifies the "king" in Balaam's prophecy as the "Seed" of Abraham. The Seed of Abraham is understood collectively at first, but he is also the individual man of promise who is to come. These literary connections and quotations in the Bible are often the most significant texts in a passage. Even so, there will be an individual coming king, who will be the focus of the patriarchal promise of God in the future.

Esau Shows Up Too Late to Be Blessed – 27:30–40

Esau appears as a tragic character; indeed, a victim of his brother's more-resourceful actions, for when Esau learned what had happened and what his brother had done to him, "he burst out with a loud and bitter cry" (v. 34), which is reminiscent of when Jacob had stolen his birthright (25:21–34). "[Jacob] has deceived," he said. Isaac replied, "I have made him lord over you and have made all his relatives his servants, and I have sustained him with grain and new wine" (v. 37). With one more attempt to get his father to bless him as well, Isaac answered his weeping son with a repeat of the central point for the third time: "You will serve your brother" (v. 40). Isaac's blessing was irrevocable, even though it was deceitfully gained. Its accomplishment is out of human hands: It will entirely be the work of God.

Jacob's Flight from Beersheba to Paddan-Aram – 27:41–28:9

Jacob ended up obtaining the blessing just as Rebekah had schemed, but it also meant he had to leave Beersheba and flee to Paddan-Aram to avoid his brother's unmitigated wrath. Esau was overheard to declare that once Isaac passed away, he would kill Jacob. Once again, Rebekah stepped in to thwart his plan by having Isaac send off Jacob to Rebekah's homeland and to her brother Laban.

Once more there is another departure, this time for Jacob to visit Laban in Haran for a while, hopefully giving enough time for Esau's bitter anger to cool. This unfortunately would be the last time Jacob would see or be with his mother, for the short time assigned to him for obtaining a wife turned out to be 20 years.

Isaac summoned Jacob to him and blessed him prior to his departure. He clearly commanded him: "Do not marry a Canaanite woman" (v. 1). Jacob was to go to his mother's father, named Bethuel, and take from that family one of Laban's daughters as a wife (v. 2). So, the blessing of Abraham will rest on Jacob:

> May God Almighty bless you and make you fruitful and increase your numbers until you become a community of peoples. May he give you and your descendants the blessing given to Abraham, so that you may take possession of the land where you now live as an alien, the Land God gave to Abraham. (vv. 3–4)

Esau, still hot under the collar for what had happened, found a way to spite his parents for what he regarded as non-support of him and his future. Esau realized it would displease his parents immensely if he married a Canaanite. So, he went to Ishmael and married Mahalath, the sister of Nebaioth and the daughter of Ishmael the son of Abraham (v. 8) in addition to the wives he already had.

As we will later see, after 20 years of separation Jacob will return, and by then Esau will have overcome his anger against his brother, for when they meet, Esau will run to meet Jacob and embrace him, throwing his arms around his neck and kissing him, and they will weep" (Gen. 33:4, 11). It was important that the men were reconciled to each other, for the future hope found later in the prophetic books—namely, that all nations and all men would seek the Lord—must come to pass (Amos 9:12; see Acts 15:17). Moreover, did not the promise of God include the fact that "all peoples on earth will be blessed through you" (Gen. 12:3)?

Conclusions

1. The home of Isaac and Rebekah was filled with a strong difference of opinion over the parental preference for a different child in that family. Isaac loved his firstborn Esau and Rebekah loved Jacob.
2. Isaac prepared to bless his eldest son Esau, but Rebekah overheard their preparations for this event, and she intervened with a scheme of her own to see that Jacob was blessed. Was her plan from God? If not, why was it approved eventually by God?
3. Jacob takes the tasty dish his mother had made to his father as he pretended to be Esau in the disguise his mother had designed.
4. When Esau learned that his brother had once again tricked him out of his blessing, he begged his father to think of some blessing for him, or to revoke what he had given to Jacob, but Isaac remained adamant that that was impossible.
5. Jacob was sent off to Haran to marry a wife from the family of Bethuel and Laban. There he served Laban to earn the bride-price and the cost of a flock and herd from Laban for 20 years.

Questions for Thought or Discussion

1. How do you answer the fact that Jacob and Rebekah used deceit and lying to obtain the promised blessing of God?
2. Was Isaac out of God's will in wanting to bless his oldest son Esau rather than Jacob?
3. Why does the Bible tell the story of a Jacob who lives up to his name of "deceiver" as part of how God will bring to pass his promise-plan? This sounds like doing evil so good may come!
4. If Isaac felt so strongly about his oldest son being the one to receive the inheritance, why did he finally pronounce the blessing on Jacob as he left for Haran?
5. Why must the family in the line of promise go at first to their relative's families for wives? Weren't there others they could have married?

Lesson 4

Jacob Flees to Haran and Marries Leah and Rachel

Genesis 28:10–29:30

Previously, we learned that the real reason for Jacob's trip to Haran was to escape Esau's wrath; he planned to murder Jacob (27:43–45). But once again Rebekah, who favored Jacob, stepped in by providing him with the excuse that she did not want Jacob to marry a Hittite woman (27:46) as Esau had done (26:34–35). This excuse, though also a concern of both Jacob's mother and father, tended to conceal the more-obvious cause for sending off her son, never to see him again.

Off went Jacob by himself to the plains of Aram or Syria, a site located in northwest Mesopotamia, where Isaac's grandfather Bethuel lived along with his uncle Laban. This journey had already been noted in 28:5, but the text picks up the story again in 28:10. Jacob journeyed along until the sun set, and there he found himself in a place apparently littered with stones. There he rested his head, using a stone as a pillow, as he settled down for the night. As he fell asleep, he had a dream, which is at the center of his journey to Haran.

Jacob Dreams at Bethel – 28:10–22

Abraham received the word of the Lord "in a vision" (15:1), while Jacob received God's word in "a dream" (v. 12). In both instances, at the center of all that is happening is the fact that God confirms the establishment of his covenant with both of them. Central to God's promise to Jacob was the word that "I [the LORD] am with you and will bring you back to this land" (v. 15). This shows that God was overseeing and making sure his plan was being carried out. Jacob showed his awareness of this point by erecting a "pillar" (Hebrew *matstsebah*) at the outset of his journey. He named the place where the dream had come to him Bethel (vv. 18–19). When he returned from Haran after 20 years of absence from the Promised Land, he erected another "pillar" and reaffirmed that the name of the place was Bethel (35:14–15).

When Jacob stopped that night in that place he would name Bethel, which formerly was called Luz, it was a rock-strewn landscape with loose boulders everywhere. He may even have found it difficult to locate a spot that was free of boulders to lie down, but he did get a spot, as he also used one of those rocks as a pillow. A hard headrest was not unusual for those days, so the boulder would suit his needs fine.

After Jacob fell asleep, he had a dream in which he saw a "stairway" that reached from heaven to earth (v. 12). This so-called "ladder" touched the ground, and its top reached the sky, perhaps somewhat like the stairs of a ziggurat, a fairly common temple tower in Mesopotamia. The people of that day had once tried to build the Tower of Babel, but the Lord confused their language. Unable to understand each other, they could not continue building (Gen. 11:9). But in Jacob's dream, there were angels of God who kept going up and down the "stairway," though their purpose is not explained.

This theme of angels ascending and descending was also used by Yeshua as he interviewed Nathaniel in John 1:51, saying, "You will see heaven open, and the angels of God ascending and descending on the Son of Man." Yeshua therefore depicted himself to Nathaniel as a bridge of sorts between heaven and earth, he who was the final and only real mediator "between God and man" (1 Timothy 2:5). At the summit of a ziggurat—a sort of stepped pyramid—was a small temple, often painted in blue enamel. But in Jacob's dream, instead of a small temple or shrine at the top, God himself stood at the top of the staircase, in stark contrast to any ziggurat (v. 13). From there he renewed the blessing previously made with Abraham and Isaac, which promised the land of Canaan to Jacob and his descendants, only this time the seed of this patriarch was likened in number to the specks of dust on the earth! (v. 14) It is interesting to observe the metaphors used to describe the numerical increase of the descendants of Israel. At first, they were said to be as numerous as the stars in the sky (15:5), which is convincing enough; on a clear night, thousands of stars dot the heavens. Later they were said to exceed the number of "grains of sand" on the shores of the earth (22:17). Finally, the number of descendants was said to be as innumerable as all the "specks of dust" on the earth (v. 14). An infinite God is just as extravagant in the extent of his blessings as well!

When Jacob awoke from his improvised bed, stretched out of the earth and the stone pillow he had laid on, he realized at once that God must have been in that place! This at first caused him some fright, for he marveled, "How awesome is this place! This is none other than the house of God; this is the gate of heaven" (v. 17). The dual name of this place as being the "house of God" and the "gate of heaven" might be a clue as to what was going on here, for "Babel" literally meant "gateway to a god." Moreover, the Tower of Babel was known as "the House of the Foundation Platform of Heaven and Earth." Thus, it might be that Jacob's description of his heavenly staircase did recall the Mesopotamian ziggurats. But instead of meeting an idol at this temple at the head of the staircase, Jacob met the Living God himself!

Jacob took the boulder he had rested upon and used it to set up a stone monument. He did this by pouring oil on the stone, to consecrate it (Exodus 30:25–29), and he named it Bethel, changing the locale's name from Luz (Gen. 28:19) to a name meaning "the house of God" (v. 17).

Jacob felt a vow to God was in order given all that had taken place here during his brief visit. In that vow, Jacob promised: "If God will be with me and will watch over me on this journey I am taking and will give me food to eat and clothes to wear so that I return safely to my father's house, then the LORD will be my God and this stone that I have set up as a pillar will be God's house, and all that you give me I will give you a tenth" (vv. 20–22). Here Jacob promised to the Lord his life, his worship, and his possessions.

Jacob Meets Rachel at the Well – Genesis 29:1–14a

The narrative continued with Jacob's journey until he came to "the land of the eastern peoples" (29:1). As we read this section, for a moment it almost seems as if we are back in time and in the land with Abraham's servant seeking a bride for Isaac (Gen. 24). However, not much space is given here for Jacob to reflect on how God had directed him across the miles to this very spot, as Abraham's servant had been so forthright in declaring; Jacob speaks barely a word in this chapter. Instead of employing camels for the trip this time, Jacob seems to set out on foot to the territory we label Qedem, meaning the "east." This label we gain from the *Story of Sinuhe*, from the days of the Twelfth Dynasty of Egypt. This document tells the story of a man named Sinuhe, who underwent voluntary exile from Egypt, and on leaving Egypt also landed in Qedem. For Jacob, this land of the "east" meant Haran (29:4).

Fortunately, at this stop there was a well, but it had a large stone over it, which the local shepherds apparently did not roll away unless there were enough present to move it. Jacob noticed that already there were "three flocks of sheep lying near [the well]" (v. 2) and that the stone over the mouth of the well was quite large indeed. The shepherds tended to wait until all the shepherds were there before they began to uncover the well and start watering the flocks.

Jacob began the conversation with the shepherds near the well: "My brothers, where are you from?" "Haran," they replied. He asked, "Do you know Laban, Nahor's grandson?" They replied, "Yes, we know him." Jacob asked, "Is he well?" The shepherds answered, "Yes, he is, and here comes his daughter Rachel with the sheep" (vv. 4–6).

But Jacob, ever the efficient administrator, instructed, "Look, the sun is still high; it is not time for the flocks to be gathered. Water the sheep and take them back to pasture" (v. 7).

"We can't," they protested, "until all the flocks are gathered and the stone has been rolled away from the mouth of the well. Then we will water the sheep" (v. 8). While he was still talking with the other shepherds, Rachel came with her father's sheep; she was a shepherdess, all right! And when he saw Laban's daughter and Laban's sheep, he went over to the well and single-handedly rolled the stone away from the mouth of the well and began to water his uncle's sheep. In the previous scene, years ago, with the servant searching for a bride for Isaac, Rebekah did all the work of fetching the water for the camels, but in this case, Jacob took care of the task of watering the flocks. I wonder what impression that made on Rachel!

"Then Jacob kissed Rachel and began to weep aloud" (v. 11). This is not surprising, given that he had successfully completed his journey to his mother's homeland, found that his relatives were just nearby, and he had seen Rachel, Laban's beautiful daughter.

Jacob disclosed that he was a relative of her uncle Laban and a son of Rebekah. Rachel was so thrilled with this news that she immediately ran to tell her father about the man she had just met. When Laban heard the good news that a relative had just come to visit them, he quickly went to meet Jacob and embraced him and kissed him. He brought Jacob home, where Jacob "told him all these things" (v. 13)—presumably, how he was related to them and how the family was doing. "You are my own flesh and blood," Laban declared (v. 14a); see Adam's similar exclamation to Eve in the Garden of Eden: "Surely you are my bone and my flesh"). Even though the text does not explicitly say so, God had providentially brought Jacob to precisely the bride he intended for him.

Jacob Marries Laban's Daughters Leah and Rachel – 29:14b–30

After Jacob had stayed with Laban for a full month, Laban magnanimously said, "Just because you are a relative of mine, should you work for me for nothing? Tell me what your wages should be" (v. 15). By this time, Jacob had fallen hopelessly in love with Laban's younger daughter Rachel. Rachel was more beautiful than her older sister Leah, whose name meant "cow's eyes." So, Jacob had a ready answer. Since he had no bride-price (Hebrew *mohar*) to pay for Rachel, he would serve Laban for seven years for her. Laban liked the terms of that deal, so it was agreed! Usually, a seven-year stretch is something drearily long and extended, but not for Jacob. Given his love for Rachel "they seemed like only a few days to him because of his love for her" (v. 20).

When the seven years had expired, Jacob announced to Laban, "Give me my wife. My time is completed, and I want to lie with her" (v. 21). That was plain enough, although with a schemer like Laban, Jacob should have included Rachel's name in the order!

Laban arranged for a marriage feast (Hebrew *mishteh*) as he brought all the people of that place together for the festivities. But when evening came, he took his daughter Leah instead of Rachel and gave her to Jacob. Laban gave a servant girl named Zilpah as a marriage gift to Leah. That night Jacob unwittingly laid with Leah, evidently thinking this was Rachel. When morning came, however, "there was Leah" (v. 25). We can imagine that a huge outcry went out from Jacob's tent. Where on earth was Laban? Jacob wanted to talk to him right now! When the two men met, Jacob demanded, "What is this you have done to me? I served you for Rachel, didn't I? Why have you deceived me?" (v. 25). But how had Jacob been tricked so badly? Was his tent too dark that night, so he didn't actually see who he was with? Was Leah's veil such that it concealed her face? Or had Jacob imbibed too much wine at the wedding feast? Or were all these contributing factors and possibly more? The text does not tell us, but one deceiver had deceived another—just as Jacob had deceived Esau, so Laban had deceived Jacob. We "reap what we have sown" (Galatians 6:7).

No doubt Jacob was fit to be tied; he must have been disgusted and mad as hops with his new father-in-law. Laban must have anticipated some of Jacob's reaction, for he had already formulated an excuse: "It is not our custom here to give the younger daughter in marriage before the older one" (v. 26). That was true, but how come he never spoke up when the deal was cut seven years before? But deceitful Laban had something else up his sleeve. Surely it was clear to him by this time that God was blessing him because of Jacob's presence and his work for him. So, Laban slyly suggested to Jacob, "Finish this daughter's bridal week; then we will give you the younger one also, in return for another seven years of work" (v. 27).

Jacob agreed, ending the crisis. He finished the bridal week with Leah, and Laban gave Jacob his daughter Rachel to be his second wife along with a marriage present of a servant girl named Bilhah. Jacob laid with both Rachel and Leah, but he loved Rachel more (v. 30a). And Jacob worked for Laban another seven years (vv. 28–30).

Conclusions

1. The dream God brought to Jacob reiterated the promise-plan that the Lord had revealed to Abraham and Isaac. It included the promise of the gift of the land, the gift of numerous descendants, and the gift of blessing all the peoples of the earth through the seed of these patriarchs.
2. Jacob vowed that if the Lord would watch over him in his journey and return him safely to his home in Canaan, then the Lord would be his God, the anointed stone he had set up would be God's house, and he would give the Lord a tenth of all he possessed!
3. The Lord providentially led Jacob to the right country, the right well, and the right girl.
4. Laban deceived Jacob by replacing Rachel with Leah as his first wife, but Jacob was enabled to work for seven more years for Rachel's hand in marriage.

Questions for Thought or Discussion

1. Did the promises God made as Jacob left home to go to Haran depend on anything he would do or contribute to this divine plan (23:13–15)?
2. How was Jacob enabled to move the stone covering the well, which usually depended on the help of several other shepherds?
3. Would you classify Rachel's turning up at the very time that Jacob arrived at the well where she ordinarily watered her father's sheep as an example of divine providence? How determinative is that analysis for our estimate of the same doctrine of "providence" in the book of Esther, where God's name is never mentioned?
4. Do you think that after the amount of time Jacob was gone from home, his mother Rebekah ever wished she had never suggested the scheme she had hatched and the absence of her son she had caused?
5. Try to imagine in your mind how Leah felt playing second fiddle to her sister in marriage and in the rest of her life!

Lesson 5

The Increase of Jacob's Family and Herds

Genesis 29:31–30:24

This chapter leads us directly to the origins of the nation of Israel, for we are taken, as it were, into the very center of Israel's first hours and the onset of her growth. This chapter also begins by telling us that it was the Lord who saw that Leah was the one who was not loved, so he intervened for her by opening her womb. As a result, she became pregnant and gave birth to Jacob's firstborn son, Reuben. Rachel, of course, was the more youthful and the one people would have naturally expected to be the more-prolific bearer of children. However, the story of this patriarchal family once again begins with the sad news that she remained childless, whereas Leah was blessed by the Lord abundantly so that she eventually became the mother of six boys! Let us look at the text itself to see how matters developed!

Leah Bears Four Sons for Jacob – 29:31–35

It is clear that the Lord took pity on Leah, as he gave her a son v. 31). This section of Genesis will tell the story of the birth of eleven of Jacob's sons. Each birth will also make evident that the Hebrew people loved wordplay, for each son's name was a pun of sorts, thus making their names easy to remember and resulting in their mother's testimony to God because of his help!

The first son born to Leah was Reuben. His name meant "See, a son!" (v. 32), but this word may have had relevance at least in relation to her husband Jacob. It is also possible that from a divine perspective, Leah meant God had "seen" her as well. It is true that she did explain part of her reason for naming her son "Reuben" was "because the LORD 'has seen' my misery." But she also was just as sure that "surely my husband will love me now" (v. 32b). But that did not prove to be the case, for Leah was still the unloved wife, despite this gift of a firstborn son!

Leah conceived a second time, and again she gave birth to a son, and she named him Simeon "because the LORD heard that I am not loved, he gave me this one too!" (v. 33) But neither did her giving birth to a second son move Jacob to love her any more than he previously had—she remained unloved!

When she gave birth to a third son, Leah thought that surely she would be able to attract her husband's love. In fact, she cried out, "Now at last my husband will become 'attached' to me, because I have borne him three sons," for that is why she named this third boy Levi. The pun on this name had the idea that now Jacob would "be "joined" or "attached" to her, but this too was wishful thinking!

Despite this outright lack of affection from Jacob, God again blessed Leah with a son. When she gave birth to a son for the fourth time, she said, "This time I will 'praise' the LORD." Thus, she named him Judah. No comment is made about Leah's relationship to Jacob because of Judah's birth, which may be because in his later years, Judah gained great prominence and rose to be one of Jacob's two most important sons.

"Then she stopped having children" (v. 35). It is impossible to tell what Leah looked like physically, but she certainly exhibited a beautiful spirit despite a father who had forced her into a situation she had not bargained for. Instead of using this fourth birth to try to win back her husband's love, she did not even bother making such a comment about her son and how it would affect Jacob's loving her; instead, she lifted her voice in "praise" to God!

Rachel Enters Her Maidservant Bilhah into the Baby Contest, Who Bears Two Sons – 30:1–7

All this time, Rachel was struggling with the fact that she was barren. As a result, she grew envious and jealous of her sister Leah. Apparently, this caused a fracture in Rachel's relationship with

Jacob, for she screamed at him, "Give me children, or I'll die!" It may be an irony or even prophetic of the fact that Rachel did die when she gave birth to her second son, Benjamin. It is clear she may have been coming to the end of her rope being barren, for she could not please her husband like her sister could by presenting him with sons. It seemed for the moment that she wanted to blame Jacob for her condition, but he became angry with her and replied, "Am I in the place of God, who has kept you from having children?" (v. 30:2)

So, a new accommodation was worked out between them. In that culture, as seen in the archaeological Nuzi documents, any children born to a handmaid of a woman were counted as the children of the woman the handmaid served. Therefore, the plan was this: Rachel would give her handmaid Bilhah to her husband to sleep with. Jacob then slept with Bilhah, and she became pregnant (vv. 3–4). Rachel received this news with joy, announcing, "God has vindicated ['done justice to'] me; he has listened to my plea and given me a son." She named him Dan. This name means "defender," or "advocate," or even "he has vindicated."

But that was not the end of this plan, for Jacob slept with Bilhah again, and again she conceived a son, whom Rachel named Naphtali (v. 7). This time Rachel punned, "I have had a great struggle [or 'have wrestled'] with my sister, and I have won" (v. 7b). Rachel may have thought her wrestling or contest was with her sister, but, her contest was with God himself. It is interesting to note that the name "Yahweh" is specifically used in connection with the first four births, but the name "Elohim" is used with the seven other sons who follow the first four.

Leah Enters Her Handmaiden Zilpah into the Baby Contest, Who Bears Two Sons – 30:9–12

Leah was beginning to feel left out, now that Rachel's handmaid had produced for her two sons who were credited to her as her own. Since Leah had stopped having children, she decided to add her servant girl, Zilpah, into this child-bearing race. She gave Zilpah to

Jacob just as Rachel had given Bilhah to him to sleep with. Zilpah then also bore to Jacob a son, whom Leah named Gad, meaning "good fortune" (vv. 10–11), which reflects Leah's cry at the birth of this son: "What good fortune!" Once more, Leah entrusted her servant girl to Jacob to sleep with, and again she bore a son. She said, "How happy I am! The women will call me happy" (vv. 12–13). Thus, she named him Asher, meaning "happy."

Leah "Rents" Her Husband Out for Reuben's Mandrakes – 30:14–16

It seems that by now Reuben was old enough to go out and play in the fields, where one day, during the wheat harvest, he found some mandrakes. He promptly and dutifully took these legendary plants to his mother Leah (v. 14). Native to the Middle East, this plant was viewed as an aphrodisiac and a fertility drug. It was not grown for food, but its root and berries were edible. Its flowers were purple, becoming dark blue in May and June, and in the days of the wheat harvest, it bears an apple-like fruit that has a distinctively pungent odor. When Rachel found out that Reuben had discovered these plants and given them to his mother Leah, Rachel pleaded, "Please give me some of your son's mandrakes" (v. 14b). Apparently, Rachel was so desperate at this point in her life that she was willing to try anything.

Leah at first reproved her sister for making such a request as she scolded, "Wasn't it enough that you took away my husband? Will you take my son's mandrakes as well?" (v. 15a) But Rachel quickly thought of a way she might work a deal. She proposed, "[Jacob] can sleep with you tonight in return for your son's mandrakes" (v. 15b). Rachel was willing to give up her turn to sleep with her husband in exchange for this supposed fertility-enhancing drug! Wow! Had Rachel, as the favorite wife, been given the dubious privilege of deciding which of Jacob's wives would sleep with him each evening? Nevertheless, as Jacob was coming in from the fields, Leah ran out to meet him and informed him she had been given that privilege of sleeping with him that evening by Rachel—all in exchange for sharing her son's mandrakes with her! Thus, Jacob slept with Leah that night (v. 16).

Leah Conceives Again and Bears Two More Sons and a Daughter, Dinah – 30:17–21

Leah must have continued to pray to God about her situation, for once more God listened to Leah and she conceived and bore her fifth child, and she commented, "God has rewarded me for giving my maidservant to my husband" (v. 17), so she named her fifth son Issachar, meaning "he has rewarded." Later, Leah bore Jacob a sixth child, saying, "God has presented me with a gracious gift. This time my husband will treat me with honor because I have borne him six sons." Leah named her sixth son Zebulun (v. 20), which probably means "honor."

Later, Leah bore a daughter, whom they named Dinah (v. 21). She was not the only daughter Jacob had, for Genesis 32:35 and 46:7 mention others. However, Dinah cannot go unmentioned, for she will become the center of attention in Genesis 34.

Rachel's Womb Is Opened and She Bears Joseph – 30:22–24

God listened to the prayer of Rachel about her barrenness and opened her womb, and she bore her first child, Joseph, saying at first, "God has taken away my disgrace," but after which she named her son "Joseph," she said, "May the LORD add to me another son." (vv. 23–24). Joseph, whose name means "may he add," was Jacob's eleventh son.

Conclusions

1. The Lord can detect when a person like Leah was not loved by her husband. Therefore, he opened Leah's womb so that she was able to give birth several times.
2. Leah named her oldest son Reuben, declaring the Lord himself had "seen" her misery. Her second son she named Simeon, because she was still sure God had "heard" that she was not loved. But it seemed as if no amount of sons she had borne to Jacob would make him love her.
3. Rachel, in desperation, demanded Jacob give her children or she would die. But Jacob fought back by asking her who did she think he was—God? The Lord, he asserted, was the One who had kept you from having children!
4. Rachel even tried using mandrakes to get pregnant, but her womb remained closed until God opened it.
5. Finally, Rachel had a son named Joseph, at which time she declared God had taken away her disgrace.

Questions for Thought or Discussion

1. Does this text support the idea that God intended Jacob to marry Leah, but Jacob wanted to marry Rachel instead, so God allowed Laban to trick him? Do you agree?
2. Did the Lord withhold "offspring" from Rachel's womb so the "seed" of Abraham would be built from Leah and not from Rachel (v. 30:2)?
3. Why is the story of the mandrakes included in this story of the birth of the children? Did this story indicate that Rachel oversaw designating who got to sleep with Jacob each night? (v. 30:15–16).
4. We are told that Leah stopped having children after she had the first four. Yet she went on to have two more sons and a daughter after she had gained that ability apparently with mandrakes from her son Reuben. Does this indicate there is anything to the mandrake's fertility power?
5. Why is the name "Yahweh" used with the birth of the first four sons born to Leah, but thereafter, the name "Elohim" is used with the next seven? Is there any reason for this distinction in the use of names for God?

Lesson 6

Jacob Agrees on a New Wage Compact and Jacob Flees from Laban

Genesis 30:25–31:21

Now that Jacob had eleven children, he pressed Laban for his dismissal from Haran. Rachel had just borne to Jacob her son Joseph, so Jacob urged Laban to send him away so he could return to his own home of Canaan. But Laban was not quite ready for such a parting, admitting that he had well observed how God had blessed him for Jacob's sake. So, he countered Jacob's request with an alternative. He urged Jacob to name what he wanted in terms of wages, and he would give him whatever he asked for. But Jacob told Laban to compare the number of sheep, goats, and cattle he owned when Jacob first came to work for him—a small number indeed, compared to how many more there had come to be during the many years of Jacob serving him day and night with all his might and with all his heart! Laban's livestock had become a veritable "multitude," for the Lord had blessed all of Jacob's efforts immensely.

Laban gave Jacob no argument over what he had said, for Laban and his sons had long since come to recognize that this was the truth—it was God who had blessed the work of Jacob for Laban. Given those terms as a background, the two men were ready to work out a new contract. Let us look at how this developed and why Jacob finally left Laban on his own initiative without his father-in-law's blessing.

Jacob Presses for His Dismissal but Instead Gets a New Contract – 30:25–31:4

Now that Jacob and Laban had finished the second seven-year contract, it was time for a new compact for the service Jacob would render to Laban. At first, Jacob pressed Laban to dismiss him. Rachel had finally been able to have a child, whom she named "Joseph," meaning he was the one that Lord had "added" to the family. But after 14 years of service, Jacob was anxious to get on the road back home. Laban was all too aware of the fact that Jacob had given him outstanding service all those years he was serving to pay the bride-price for his two daughters.

But Laban pleaded with Jacob to reconsider his desire to pack up and leave, begging him to stay "if I have found favor in your eyes" (v. 27). In a rare moment of asking Jacob to name the terms of his employment, the deceitful bargainer must have felt Jacob was quite serious about deciding to leavearan, so he put forth his best possible offer and behavior (v. 28). Laban said he would pay whatever price Jacob named! Laban had learned—by "divination," he said—that all during these years, there was a reason he was prospering. Because of Jacob's work for him, he had been blessed by God.

Jacob agreed with Laban's analysis, for Jacob called to his father-in-law's attention that when he had arrived, Laban had very little by way of livestock. But in the interim, the Lord had blessed wherever Jacob had been put in charge of Laban's operations. From here on out, though, Jacob wanted to do something on his on and for his own household (v. 30). He wanted to build his own herd and flock as well as his own house.

Jacob Resorts to Two Stratagems to Increase His Flock – 30:31–43

Surprisingly, Laban did not resist or oppose Jacob's demand for a new set of terms for his employment, simply stating, "Agreed. Let it be as you said" (v. 34). But Jacob was not looking for a handout from Laban; he was willing to work for all he would get, so he told Laban he did not want him to give him anything as a free gift (v.

31b). Jacob's action here is reminiscent of Abraham's refusal to accept any of the booty from his conquest of the four Mesopotamian kings he overtook at Dan (Gen. 14:21). God alone would get the credit for any prospering that occurred! God had likewise prospered Jacob's forerunners Abraham and Isaac (see Gen. 21:22, 26:28).

These were the terms Jacob drew up: He would personally tend Laban's flock and continue to take them under his care. But from that day on, Laban himself would pick out and remove from his own flock all the speckled or spotted sheep and goats, speckled along with every black lamb, and they would be Jacob's wages (v. 32). This seemed to be a good deal for old conniving Laban, for the sheep in that part of the world are principally white; only a few, mostly rams, are black, and the goats are generally dark-colored and very seldom white or spotted. Judging by what we know, Jacob did not land a good bargain, for he was offering his services at a very small wage, given the predominant color pattern of the flocks in that part of the world! If any goat, sheep, or lamb in Jacob's flock did not meet these new color conditions, then Laban could accuse Jacob of stealing whenever Laban checked the color tone of Jacob's flock.

Crafty Laban must have smiled to himself that Jacob had driven a bad bargain as far as his wages were concerned, for Jacob would still be in charge of his flock and herd, and God would continue to bless Laban's possessions. To ensure there was no cheating in the meantime, Jacob placed a three-day journey between Laban's herd and Jacob's newly formed one, which Laban's sons would care for. The three-day separation was meant to prevent any copulation between the normally colored and the abnormally spotted cattle. It seemed Laban was going to win big-time!

Jacob had two schemes up his sleeve, for he thought he could use a type of prenatal influence to change the color balance in the herds.

Jacob had already formulated a plan for breeding speckled and spotted animals by placing in front of them at their watering troughs three types of stripped-bark tree branches, from poplar, almond, and plane trees. Jacob would cut white stripes in the bark of these trees, thereby exposing the white inner wood, and then he would place these rods in front of the stronger animals, which would mate while the females were trying to drink water from the trough filled with these stripped rods (v. 37).

Jacob had a second strategy: He would lay down these rods of branches in the gutters of the watering troughs in front of the sheep so they might mate in front of the rods (vv. 40–41). But he wouldn't do so for the weaker sheep. Thus "the weak animals went to Laban and the strong ones to Jacob" (v. 42). This meant Jacob would lay down the rods in the summer, so the strong, unusually spotted sheep would be born as winter lambs. The weaker lambs would be spring lambs that would belong to Laban. In this way, Jacob figured, he was affecting a huge increase in his lots. Jacob grew exceedingly prosperous as he came to own a huge flock, along with maidservants and menservants, camels, and donkeys (v. 30:43).

Laban and His Sons' Attitudes Toward Jacob Change, So the Lord Calls Jacob to Return to His Own Land – 31:1–9

By this time, Jacob had been living in Paddan-Aram for some twenty years (vv. 38, 41). He had married Laban's two daughters Leah and Rachel, and along with them he had acquired two concubines. He had become the father of eleven sons and one daughter. Now he was accumulating tremendous wealth flocks and herds. But Jacob, in recent days, had overheard Laban's sons complaining about Jacob's new wage arrangement: "Jacob has taken everything our father owned and has gained all this wealth from what belonged to our father" (v. 31:1). This, of course, severely reduced what they would therefore inherit. Jacob also noticed that the attitude of his father-in-law had likewise changed, for it was not what it had been like in former times (v. 2). It was at this time that the Lord himself explained to Jacob, "Go back to the land of your fathers and your relatives, and I will be with you" (v. 3).

Jacob sent word to his wives Leah and Rachel to come out into the fields where his flocks were to meet with him, for he wanted to tell them his feelings about Laban and his sons' attitude toward him. Jacob made quite a case for the way he had served their father:

> I see that your father's attitude toward me is not what it was before, but the God of my father has been with me. You know I have worked for your father with all my strength, yet your father has cheated me by changing my wages ten times. However, God has not allowed him to harm me. If he said, the speckled ones will be your wages, then all the flocks gave birth to speckled young; and if he said, 'The streaked ones shall be your wages,' then all the flocks bore streaked young. So, God has taken away your father's livestock and given it to me. (vv. 31:5–9)

Despite all Laban's contract-maneuvering, God had still seen to it that Jacob would be blessed and not harmed. There is here also an acknowledgement that Jacob's schemes were not what was actually at work; it was all the blessing and work of God himself that was causing all Jacob's blessing! God had overruled both Jacob and Laban to ensure Jacob was the object of the divine work and blessing, just as his promise-plan had promised.

In a Dream, Jacob Is Shown That the Lord Is the One Blessing Him – 31:10–13

In the breeding season, Jacob one day dreamed of seeing that "the male goats mating with the flock were striped, speckled or dappled" (v. 10). Then he heard the "angel of God" call out his name. "Here am I," Jacob replied. The angel pointed out that all the male goats were leaping on the striped, speckled or spotted sheep (v. 12). They were doing this, God said, because of all that Laban had been doing to him (v. 12b). God identified himself as "the God of Bethel, of the place where you anointed a pillar with oil and where you made a vow to me" (v. 13; see Gen. 28:12, 17–19). God instructed Jacob to leave this land immediately and go back to his native land (v. 13b).

Perhaps by now Jacob was finally realizing that his success was not caused by his own efforts or scheme to gain an advantage over Laban, but rather that it all had happened because of God's providence and plan.

Rachel and Leah Have No Share in Their Marriage Portions – 31:14–16

Rachel and Leah said they felt that they too had been cheated, for they had been given no portion of the value derived from the 14 years of work Jacob put into Laban's herd to pay for his lack of a bride-price. This bride-price would come to the two girls if Jacob died prematurely and left them with nothing. At least they would have the bride-price. So, Laban's daughters were disgusted with his unethical ways, just as Jacob had been. The two wives asked rhetorically, didn't they have a portion in Jacob's estate? Why had he regarded them as if they were foreigners? Their father had, in effect, sold them to Jacob, then used up all that had been paid for them! (v. 15) As far as Rachel and Leah were concerned, all the wealth God had taken away from their father belonged to them and their children (v. 6). The two of them were more than ready to leave and go to Canaan.

However, just as Rebekah before them (Gen. 24:58) and Ruth after them (Ruth 1:16), Rachel and Leah were willing to leave family and friends to go to a foreign land with their husband Jacob.

Jacob Crosses the Euphrates and Heads for Gilead – 31:17–21

Jacob put his children and wives on the backs of the camels and drove the livestock ahead of them as he headed out to cross the Euphrates, which would be no small task. Jacob chose this time for his exit from Paddan-Aram, for Laban and his sons had gone off in the fields to shear the sheep. *In those days,* all sheep-shearing seemed to be celebrated in the land as a time of rustic, festive days (see 2 Samuel 13:23). That meant Laban and his men would be occupied for several days, thereby giving Jacob a good head-start on their trip and an opportunity to cross the wide Euphrates River. So, Jacob left as he wanted to—secretly and suddenly.

Rachel must have slipped back into their house before leaving, for she stole her father's "household gods" (v. 19). It seems these idols were used both for worship and as a sort of ownership symbol of all Laban's possessions. She surely thought he owed her as much, for he had used up the bride-price Jacob had paid for both of them, so it was theirs due to Laban's thievery. She didn't regard them as gods or worship them as Laban did; she was interested only in their value as a statement of the inheritance of her father's property.

There is no indication that Laban ever gave up his pagan ways and his worship or service of these idols. This may explain why he handled his business matters in such an unjust and unrighteous way.

Conclusions

1. With Rachel finally giving birth to Joseph, Jacob wanted to return to Canaan. However, he was persuaded by Laban to remain for what turned out to be another six years.
2. The compact Jacob and Laban drew up was one where Jacob continued to care for Laban's herd, but Laban's sons would tend Jacob's new herd, which would consist of all the stripped, spotted, and speckled sheep and goats.
3. Jacob tried to artificially increase the number of the flock he would get by a superstitious method of prenatal influence on the females as they mated at the watering troughs, but all along it was God's blessing, not Jacob's schemes, that was resulting in the wealth of his possessions.
4. God appeared to Jacob in a dream during breeding season and said he had seen how badly Laban had treated him. It was now time for Jacob and his family to return to Canaan.
5. Rachel stole the household gods, symbols of Laban's ownership. But even as she tried to take matters into her own hands, it was God who would continue to bless them so they could be a blessing to all the peoples of the earth.

Questions for Thought or Discussion

1. Do you think God was trying to teach Jacob, during those 20 years he served deceitful Laban, that deception is wrong and unjust?
2. Why do you think Laban changed Jacob's wages ten different times? What was God doing on Joseph's behalf that may have caused such action on Laban's part?
3. Was it just or fair for Jacob to try to breed the stronger sheep with his schemes, or should he have bred all of Laban's flock by the same measure?
4. Despite what Jacob thought he was doing for himself, all along God was fabulously blessing him. Does this sound like any of the things we do to make our situations look better when it is God who is really blessing us?
5. Should Rachel have stolen the household gods of Laban even if she did not use them for worship, but only as a signal of the will she had been cheated out of?

Lesson 7

Laban Catches Up with Jacob and Rebukes Him

Genesis 31:22–55

This climactic chapter, featuring the final interaction between Jacob and Laban in their quarter-century-long relationship, opens with Laban pursuing Jacob (vv. 22–23). The chase closes with a peaceful parting of the two men and families, who apparently would never again see each other this side of eternity. In between these two bracketing events of the chase and the agreeing to the Mizpah Benediction is the unusual divine dream-warning that God gives to pagan Laban to say nothing good or bad (v. 24), after which a covenant is made between Laban and Jacob (vv. 45–54).

Laban Chases Jacob and Gets a Warning from God – 31:22–25

Jacob deceived Laban by not telling him he was permanently leaving his household and his employ; he simply picked up and left without giving any notice. He would cross over the mighty Euphrates River and then head south to Gilead, a territory northeast of the Sea of Galilee. When Laban heard the news that Jacob had skipped town, it was three days after he had left Haran. So, Laban took his relatives and some men and set out in pursuit of Jacob's entourage. He finally caught up with him seven days later, in the hill country of Gilead (vv. 22–23a).

God came to Laban the Aramean in a dream. The one omnipotent God warned this polytheist, "Be careful not to say anything to Jacob either good or bad" (v. 24). This dream-revelation was surprising, for there is no evidence that Laban had given up worship of his pagan gods—the gods of Nahor!

Finally, Jacob was able to pitch his tent in the hill country of Gilead, but that is where Laban overtook him after his seven-day journey.

An Eloquent Reproof, a Divine Reminder, and a Lame Excuse – 31:26–32

Laban had been directly warned by God to behave toward Jacob in a passive, non-aggressive manner, which is best understood to mean that he was not to be hostile as he questioned or reproached him. Therefore, Laban began his questioning of Jacob in this manner:

> "What have you done? You've deceived me, and you've carried off my daughters like captives in war. Why did you run off secretly and deceive me? Why didn't you tell me, so I could send you away with joy and singing to the music of tambourines and harps? You didn't even let me kiss my grandchildren and my daughters good-bye. You have done a foolish thing. I have the power to harm you; but last night the God of your father said to me, 'Be careful not to say anything to Jacob, either good or bad.' Now you have gone off because you longed to return to your father's house. (vv. 26–30a)

Twice in this speech Laban used the Hebrew word *ganab*, meaning "to steal, cheat" or "to slip away stealthily" (vv. 26, 27). In Laban's estimation, Jacob had "acted foolishly" (v. 28); he thought Jacob had violated a kinship ethos and acted duplicitously (see 29:26). But even more tellingly, v. 29 reads literally: "It is in the god of my hand to do you harm." In saying this, Laban appears to refer to his own personal family idol-god and not the Almighty God of Abraham, Isaac, and Jacob. But it was the God of Jacob's father, the Lord himself, who had stayed his hand.

Laban asked Jacob why he had stolen his goods, and Jacob's reply echoed Abraham's answer to Abimelech (20:11). But when Laban charged Jacob and his household with stealing his household gods (v. 31:30b), Jacob pronounced a death sentence on anyone in his group who might have taken these idols. He was certain he taken nothing from Laban, having instead worked for all he got in the blessing of God. Had he known it was his beloved Rachel who had stolen the household gods, it would have shocked him greatly—especially considering his condemning that person to death! The Hebrew verb *ganab* appears seven times (vv. 30:33; 31:19, 20, 26, 27, 30, 32). Had Rachel's theft been discovered, she would have been a victim of her father's rash oath just as Judge Jephthah's daughter was (Judges 11:29–40).

It is fascinating to see Rachel through the eyes of her husband, for we might ask how she learned such deceitful ruses; were these learned from Jacob's actions? Imagine how effective Rachel's excuse was as she protested that she could not get down from her camel because she was having her period. Did this mean these idols had also become unclean, since they were in the saddle she was sitting on? Moreover, was she telling the truth about her condition, or was she lying? However, her reluctance ultimately spared the life of Benjamin and all the descendants of his tribe! Except for God's grace, there is no other explanation to such questions. Such a vow, however, always is very dangerous!

Jacob does offer what seems a rather lame excuse: "I was afraid, because I thought you would take your daughters away from me by force" (v. 31). Yes, Laban was indeed deceitful, but there is no evidence that he would snatch his daughters and grandchildren by force! And for good measure, Jacob added, "But if you find anyone who has your gods, he shall not live" (v. 32a), for Jacob did not know that Rachel had stolen Laban's gods. Laban systematically began the search!

The Search for Laban's Household Gods – 31:33–35

Jacob gave Laban permission to look though all their belongings, so he went first into Jacob's tent. But he found nothing. Laban proceeded to search Leah's tent, then two maidservants' tents, but again he came up empty (v. 33). Finally, he searched Rachel's tent. She had indeed removed the *teraphim*—the "household gods"—from Laban's home, but she had put them inside of her camel's saddle and was now sitting on them (v. 34). She said she was having her period and could not get down from her camel (v. 35).

There is some wry humor here, for Laban's false gods are so small and helpless that they can be hidden in a camel's saddle and sat upon! They also were now useless, since a menstruating woman had rendered them unclean! (Lev. 15:20)

Jacob's Eloquent Rebuttal to Laban's Fruitless Search, and a Covenant to Follow – 31:36–45

It was now Jacob's turn to be angry, for he began by charging Laban with making a false accusation, as he started to lay out his case, so the kinfolks who were gathered there could make a "decision" (*hokiah*, "to decide a case") between the two men (vv. 36–37). Jacob continued by accusing Laban of getting the better part of every deal they had made for the last 20 years (vv. 36–41). Jacob concluded his tirade thus: "If the God of my father, the God of Abraham and the fear of Isaac, had not been with me, you would surely have sent me away empty-handed" (v. 42). That must have hurt Laban badly, but it seems it was true!

Jacob referred to God as "the God of my father" in 31:5, and Laban, in speaking to Jacob, had referred to "the God of your father" in 31:29. Now in 31:42 Jacob identified him more specifically as "the God of Abraham and the Fear of Isaac" (see also v. 53). What sense, or meaning, should we give to this unusual title? The best meaning seems to be "the revered One," for it points to God's holiness, transcendence, and otherness. But if the word means "kinsman," as W. F. Albright rendered it,[1] then the term points to God's closeness,

---

1. William Foxwell Albright, *From the Stone Age to Christianity*, 2nd edition (Baltimore: Johns Hopkins Press, 1957), 248.

his nearness, or his immanence. It was this God who had seen the hardships Jacob had to endure for the past 26 years (v. 42).

Laban was not an easy man to deal with. Instead of acknowledging some or all of Jacob's points, he raised the stakes even higher, boldly asserting:

> The women are my daughters, the children are my children, and the flocks are my flocks. All you see is mine. Yet what can I do today about these daughters of mine, or about the children they have borne? (v. 43)

From Laban's point of view, he owned everything in Jacob's possessions, including his daughters, grandchildren, and flocks. Laban did concede, however, that the daughters were within their rights to follow their husband back to Canaan (v. 43). So, to settle things, Laban proposed the two of them make a covenant to function as a witness between both of them (v. 44).

Jacob Sets Up Another Memorial Pillar Ending with the Mizpah Benediction – 31:45–50

This covenant turned out to be a non-aggression pact in which both Laban and Jacob promised not to deceive each other any longer and not to trespass on each other's territory (vv. 50–51). To mark this boundary between them, Jacob again took a large rock and set it up as a pillar. Then he instructed his relatives to gather up stones and pile them in a heap. After the stones had formed a mound, both men gave the pillar and mound a name. Laban called it Jegar-Sahadutha, and Jacob called it Galeed, meaning "witness heap" in Aramaic and Hebrew, respectively. Laban declared: "This heap is a witness between you and me today" (v. 48). Then we are told that this is why Jacob also called the heap Galeed.

This pillar was also known as Mizpah, meaning "watchtower," calling forth Laban's comment, which became known as the Mizpah

Benediction: "May the LORD keep watch between you and me when we are away from each other" (v. 49). This benediction became known in some churches as the "Mizpah Benediction," and it was oftentimes used by Christian groups invoking something very positive, blessing each other while they were apart from each other. In my early years, I was an active part of a national organization called the "Christian Endeavor." At the end of each meeting, all the young people gathered for our C.E. meeting repeated the Mizpah Benediction, praying as conscientiously as we could. Even though in its original context this benediction was made between two deceptive men who didn't trust each other, for us it was a positive and heartfelt blessing.

A Future Function of the Pillar Guaranteed Not by the Pagan God of Nahor, but by Jacob's Sacrifice to the Lord – 31:51–55

Jacob swore by the "Fear of his father Isaac," which reflects God's interaction with him in Genesis 28:11–22. Accordingly, Isaac's God is the God of Abraham, who was prompted by providence through Isaac, rather than Esau, to bless Jacob, and to receive the blessings recorded in Genesis 27:28–29 and 28:3–4. As Jacob was taking leave to go home, he swore an oath that called to mind the one he had sworn to God as he started out on this journey 26 years ago. This oath he swore in the name of the "Fear of his father Isaac" (v. 54). As he now lives by these two oaths, one to God and one to Laban, Jacob will become in fact and in reality, the "Man of Completion" (Hebrew *ish tam*), which he was said to be in principle in 25:27.

O.T. Allis wrote a brief article on "the Fear of Isaac" wherein he located Isaac's title for God in the experience of Isaac himself. He wrote:

> It seems remarkable that no attempt has been made to connect these words, the Fear of Isaac, with that tragic experience of Isaac's youth on Mt. Moriah, when his father all but offered him as a sacrifice upon the altar, in obedience to Jehovah's command. From the standpoint of a sound psychology, it is certain that this awful ordeal must have made a deep and lasting impression upon his mind, especially since it occurred in the most impressionable period of his life. … And nothing was more obviously calculated to stamp deeply upon the soul of Isaac the thought of the awful righteousness and severity of God than the fearful testing of his father's faith and his own filial obedience, which there took place."[2]

These three names are used for God by the patriarchs: "The God of Abraham" (*'elohe 'abraham*), "The Fear of Isaac" (*pahad yishaq*), and "The Mighty One of Jacob" (*'abhir ya`aqob*), especially from Gen. 49:24. But contrary Albrecht Alt's famous 1968 essay "The God of the Fathers," in which he argued that the *'elim* functioned only as appellatives in the divine names (as e.g. in El-Elyon, which he claimed stood for the "god Elyon") and were not used as proper names, as conservatives argue. But Thomas Edward McComiskey rebutted that conclusion: "There is good evidence for regarding the God of the patriarchs [by the] name El, who manifested various aspects of his nature in the epithets by which He is known."[3] These epithets "may well be descriptive epithets of El, the God of the patriarchs."

---

2. Oswald T. Allis, "The Fear of Isaac," *The Princeton Theological Review* XVI (1918): 302.
3. Thomas E. McComiskey, "The Religion of the Patriarchs: An Analysis of *The God of the Fathers* by Albrecht Alt," in *The Law and the Prophets*, ed. John H. Skilton (Phillipsburg, NJ: Presbyterian & Reformed Publishing Co., 1974), 204, 206.

Conclusions

1. Jacob got a three-day jump on his uncle Laban as he fled from him place in Haran to the land of Canaan.
2. Laban overtook him seven days later in Gilead and decried Jacob's actions of leaving his employ without giving any notice.
3. Rachel stole Laban's household gods. These small items, which could fit in her camel's saddle, were not only the deities he worshiped, but also proof of ownership of the inheritance for all Laban possessed.
4. Jacob once again set up a pillar as he had when he left Canaan 26 years before and this pillar and a heap of stones about it was called "Mizpah."
5. The two men swore the Mizpah Benediction, which said: "May the LORD keep watch between you and me when we are away from each other."

Questions for Thought or Discussion

1. What are your thoughts on the fact that the God of Abraham, Isaac, and Jacob came to polytheistic Laban in a dream with a message about his treatment of Jacob? Does God talk to unconverted pagans?
2. Laban complained that Jacob had deceived him in making off with his daughters and grandchildren. He claimed that he owned them along with everything else Jacob had. Do you think his claim was true?
3. Jacob's response to his father-in-law's charges was that he feared Laban would take from him his wives and children. Was this a valid excuse?
4. Do you think that Rachel actually had her period, or was she lying?
5. Of what value do you think the pillar was as a witness between two men who had regularly deceived each other up to that point?

Lesson 8

Jacob Sends a Gift to His Brother Esau and Wrestles With a "Man" at Peniel

Genesis 32:1–32

As Jacob went on his way to Canaan, the angels of God met him. When he saw these angels, he declared: "This is the camp of God!" (v. 1). Jacob recognized God had given him a heavenly escort by means of this angelic host. He named the place Mahanaim, meaning "two camps." It was in the territory of the tribe of Gad, just north of the Jabbok River in Transjordania, a city that later was identified as a Levite city. The name of this city was also inscribed upon one of the Karnak Tablets concerning the march of Shishak, who attacked Judah in 925 B.C.E.

But Jacob's real concern, even with the assurances of an angelic escort on his trip home after a 26-year absence, was how his brother would react once they met again. Esau, it turned out, was dwelling in the land of Seir, but Jacob sent messengers to tell Esau he was on his way home. With that, Esau headed out to meet Jacob (v. 6). Did he have scouts who had picked up this news from observing local traffic on the international trade routes? What was Jacob to do? He had been assured of God's presence, protection, and blessing, but how would that, with what seemed likely to happen next—if his scouts were correct in reporting that Esau had 400 men with him—ease Jacob's mind about what might unfold next? This sets the stage for our study!

Jacob Sends Messengers to Esau, Who Learns He is on His Way to Meet Him – 32:3–6

Given the rather large number of miles between where Jacob presently was and where Esau was living, it is surprising that word got to Esau that Jacob was on his way home. After Jacob had sent messengers with this word for Esau, his estranged brother decided to go meet him! This, then, is what the messengers found out, which his men must have reported back to Esau, while Jacob's scouts or messengers were telling him the same thing.

The presence of the angelic host that now accompanied Jacob must have comforted and reassured him along the lines that the psalmist had written in Psalm 34:7, "The angel of the LORD encamps around those who fear him, and he delivers them." What a promise—not only for Jacob and his descendants, but also for the people of God.

Jacob seemed to leave few things to chance; as always, he was a planner. Knowing Esau was on his way to meet Jacob with 400 men, Jacob instructed his messengers:

> "This is what you are to say to my lord Esau: 'Your servant Jacob says, I have been staying with Laban and have remained there till now. I have cattle and donkeys, sheep and goats, menservants and maidservants. Now I am sending this message to my lord, that I may find favor in your eyes.'" (32:4–5)

It was necessary for Jacob to settle some old accounts with his estranged brother before he could feel safe and at home in the land of Canaan once again. Jacob had cheated Esau, the firstborn in the family, out of both his birthright and his blessing. There was little doubt that Jacob had left Canaan with a tainted past—one filled with deceit and treachery. His sin against his brother and God had to be made right before the Lord, for if he thought he could rest comfortably in the land without some form of reconciliation, he was mistaken. Likewise, our fellowship with God will remain fractured if we leave unreconciled agenda on the plate from our past actions as we hopelessly attempt to gain God's favor!

Jacob Divides His Entourage into Two Groups – 32:7–9

Jacob, also being a man of this world, understood that the brother he had stolen from might still be angry. He decided to take some precautions, even to the point of separating his entourage into two groups, so that if one was attacked, the other group might be able to escape. However, Jacob realized that even these preventions were not in and of themselves sufficient. Despite such prudent measures, Jacob felt in some ways a very dark future might lie ahead of him. This hurdle was best met by believing prayer, so he prayed to God in his moment of deep need.

Jacob Asks God to Remember His Promise to Him – 32:10–13

This prayer was the second recorded one Jacob prayed during his days involved with Laban; his first such prayer was in Gen. 28:22. Here Jacob prayed for mercy and guidance, reminding God that he was the One who had advised him to return to the land of Canaan (31:13), and he was the One who had promised he would bear a great many descendants (v. 12). Jacob found himself in a time of deep trouble in this situation, so in such a difficult time, he went immediately to God in prayer and laid out his problem.

God had promised that he surely would do Jacob good. It's not as if God disliked being reminded of his promises; it was simply a call for God to be true to his word. After all, what else did Jacob have to rely on except the word of God? And by what other means could he realize what God had said than by coming to him in prayer? Prayer was the best and preferred avenue in times like these!

A Gift for Esau Is Out in Front of the Two Groups with Jacob – 32:14–22

Jacob really piled on the size of his gift to Esau. It was enormous. It included 200 female goats, 20 male goats, 200 ewes, 20 rams, 30 milk camels with their foals, 40 cows, 10 bulls, 20 female donkeys, and 10 males. This proportion of ten to one in his selection of male and male animals is noteworthy, for it provided the option for Esau of increasing the number of his animals by breeding all these Jacob had delivered to him.

A "Man" Wrestles with Jacob at Peniel – 32:23–32

Jacob sent members of his immediate family across the Jabbok River (now called the Wadi Zarqa, a seasonal stream that flows into the Jordan River some 20 miles north of the Dead Sea). There Jacob found himself alone wrestling with a "man" (v. 24) in a match that lasted all night and did not end until daybreak. Hosea 12:3–4 clearly identifies Jacob's opponent as God himself, or a person of angelic origins, one who had the authority of a divine messenger. The wrestling match, strange in almost any way one could describe it, however, ended with neither man able to declare victory! The person with supernatural credentials was able to dislocate Jacob's hip in this all-night match (v. 25), thus causing him to walk with a limp from that time onward (v. 31). What was injured seemed to be the tendon that served the sciatic muscle from his hip down his leg, which led to the dietary prohibition for all Israelites from that time forward to not eat the hip muscle of any animal (v. 32).

Jacob refused to release the man until the angel—or whoever it was who was wrestling with him—would bless him (vv. 26, 29). After blessing Jacob, this man changed Jacob's name (which meant "deceiver") to "Israel," meaning "God struggles" or "he struggles with God." This name change was because Jacob had indeed struggled, at least in one way or another, with God, and he had emerged undefeated (v. 28). This name change is again mentioned in Gen. 35:10; as well, this name was repeated in later generations of Israelites (1 Kings 18:31; 2 Kings 17:34). But at the same time, Jacob had become, by name and by the history of that nation, "Israel."

After receiving his new name, Jacob asked his opponent what his name was, but he refused to identify himself (v. 29). This same situation would be repeated in the time of the Judges when the angel of the Lord was asked an identical question about his name (Judges 13:17–18); on that occasion, the angel replied that his name was "wonderful" (or "beyond understanding"), perhaps signaling that the Almighty was in this messenger, authenticating his message!

Jacob called the name of this place Peniel, meaning "face of God." We are not certain where Peniel is located, but it can't have been far from the Jabbok River. Jacob, however, who thought he had seen the face of God, was surprised that he was still alive (v. 30), as happened in other situations (Judges 6:22, 13:22). But what these situations point to is the fact that Scripture routinely says that God is Spirit and therefore has no physical form or characteristics (John 4:24). As such, no one could see God's face and still live (Exod. 33:20). However, there were occasions where mortals saw God's "feet" (Exod. 24:10) or his "form" (Num. 12:8).

Jacob shows us from his experience at Peniel what persistence in prayer and constancy in faith looks like! Jacob was relentless in his struggle with Laban and apparently fearless in his "struggle" with God. In like manner, so it will be with our own lives: They will be strengthened and spiritually enlivened by persistent prayer and a valiant faith in God.

Conclusions

1. On two different occasions Jacob meets and must deal with angels as he returned to the land of Canaan. They play a huge role in his return!
2. Jacob instructed the messengers of each of the three groups of animals that formed Esau's gift to use the same subservient language. When they spoke to his brother Esau, they were to use expressions such as "my lord Esau," and "your servant Jacob."
3. Jacob described himself as being unworthy of all the kindnesses and faithfulness the Lord had shown to him. When he began his journey to Haran, he had only a staff, but now on his return he had become so prosperous that he was able to form them into two groups.
4. When Jacob sent all his groups across the Jabbok River, he was left alone to wrestle with a man all night until daybreak. The prophet Hosea identified that person as "God!"
5. God changed Jacob's name from meaning a "deceiver" to the name "Israel," meaning "he who struggles with God and men."

Questions for Thought or Discussion

1. What role do the angels play in Jacob's return to the land of Canaan?
2. Do you find in Jacob's prayer to God any evidence of a humble attitude about his own present abilities vis-à-vis what God had done for him since he left home?
3. Was the "man" who wrestled with Jacob a man, an angel, or God himself? Give evidence for your position.
4. Why did the Lord change Jacob's name? What was the significance of such a change?
5. What is the significance of God causing Jacob to limp because of his hip being divinely touched near his tendon?

Lesson 9

Jacob's Meeting with Esau and Arrival at Shechem

Genesis 33:1–20

Jacob looked up to see his estranged brother Esau approaching with 400 men. To prepare for this encounter, Jacob had divided his entourage into three separate groups—in front of the group, his maidservants and their children; in the next line, Leah and her children; and in the rear, Rachel, with her son Joseph (vv. 1–2).

Jacob, however, went ahead of the three groups, and he bowed down to the ground seven times as he drew near to his brother. Surely, this was a bold sign of genuine humility. This approach of superabundant courtesy was not a false or hypocritical act, for Jacob knew he had sinned greatly against his brother, so such an external act was necessary to show his internal repentance as he recalled all his faults and the devious ways he had treated his brother. The narrative here is one of the great stories of forgiveness and reconciliation in the Bible. Let us examine it more closely.

Jacob Prepares for the Worst as He Meets Esau –33:1–3

Neither we the readers nor Jacob were prepared for the greeting Jacob was about to receive. Given what had taken place between the brothers twenty-six years before, when Jacob left home, he likely expected his brother to take revenge. Jacob had more than one reason to expect some type of fireworks from Esau; for when he had last left him, Esau was threatening to murder him right after their father Isaac died, had not Jacob's mother Rebekah intervened and sent Jacob off to live in Syria with her parents.

To reiterate, Jacob bravely put himself at the head of his traveling group, and when he finally caught sight of his brother, Jacob reverentially bowed down to the ground seven times to Esau. Jacob's fears were well-founded. But what Jacob could not have anticipated was that Esau had had quite a change of heart.

Esau Breaks the Ice by Embracing His Brother and Asking How Jacob's Entourage Was Related to Him – 33:4–7

The change of attitude between the brothers was dramatically depicted. Esau's eager excitement at seeing his brother Jacob, after being separated from him for so long, evidenced itself by Esau's action of running to meet his brother, embracing, and kissing him. That must have blown away Jacob, for given the elaborate contingency plans Jacob had made, Esau's joy at meeting him was completely unanticipated. Even though there would continue to be resentment between the nations of Israel and Edom, whose opposition descended from the two brothers, and even though at times God used Edom to chastise his sinning people of Israel, eventually God's kingdom was beautifully and graciously extended to include Edom (Obadiah 21).

In the Hebrew text there are six diacritic marks in v. 4—"he kissed [*nashaq*] him," which generally means the Jewish scribes thought a word was missing from some of the Hebrew manuscripts and from the Greek Septuagint. The Jewish Midrash, however, took these six marks or dots as a mark of interrogation, meaning they had a doubt about the sincerity of the "kissing" and preferred to read "he bit him" instead of "he kissed him." But that may come from the national hostility that continued to breach the two peoples of a relationship that God promised to heal by the final day.

Esau was impressed by the identity and the large number of women and children that accompanied his brother, so he asked who they were and why were they with Jacob (v. 5). Jacob's response was one that gave glory to God; he simply answered: "These are the children God (literally "Elohim") has graciously given your servant" (v. 5b). Some think Jacob purposely suppressed the name "Yahweh" at this point for his more-secular brother Esau's sake.

Esau Questions the Need of a Gift from Jacob – 33:8–11

Esau had another question: What was the meaning of the company of the five droves of animals he had met on his way prior to meeting with Jacob (v. 8)? Jacob explained that they were so that he would be able to find favor in the eyes of his brother (v. 8b). But Esau protested that he already had enough livestock, so Jacob should keep those animals for himself (v. 9). But Jacob quickly retorted:

> "No, please! If I have found favor in your eyes, accept this gift from me. For to see your face is like seeing the face of God, now that you have received me favorably. Please accept the present that was brought to you, for God has been gracious to me and I have all I need." (vv. 10–11)

When Jacob said that seeing Esau's face was "like seeing the face of God," he likely meant that seeing his brother's face in such hospitable circumstances was like heaven itself smiling upon him! His brother's attitude and disposition toward him had changed remarkably beyond all expectations he had or he even could have imagined! The Lord was the God who had heard his prayers, and he was the God who worked on the hearts of men. Did not Psalm 33:15 teach:

> "[The LORD was the One] who forms the hearts of all, who considers everything they do."

Jacob gave two reasons why his brother should accept his gift: (1) his gift was an expression of a wish for a blessing from God to rest on his relative, and (2) Jacob now had all he needed! Both statements were testimonies to the ancient, promised blessing that would come from the hand of God. So, because Jacob insisted, Esau accepted this gift from his brother (v. 11b).

Esau Offers to Escort Jacob and His Cattle Home – 33: 12–15

Esau urged Jacob to accept his generous offer to escort him and his cattle to where he was going, but Jacob declined. This was not because Jacob felt unsafe in Esau's presence, but it was an indication that he, who now held the blessing of the birthright, did not want to involve himself in any new obligation to his brother. Just as his grandfather Abraham refused to accept any portion of the loot taken from the five kings of Mesopotamia, so Jacob would likewise maintain his independence from all mortals. Everything he had would come from the Lord, who promised to bless him. Moreover, given all the young animals with him, he could not drive them to match Esau's marching pace, who apparently was not thus encumbered. Even when Esau offered to leave a portion of his 400 men to help drive the herds for Jacob, Jacob still courteously turned down that offer as well (v. 15).

Esau Journeys on to Seir and Jacob to Succoth and Shechem – 33:16–20

The Succoth mentioned here must have been the Succoth that was on the east side of the Jordan, which laid between the Jabbok River and the high road that led from Al-Salt in Gilead to Shechem in Canaan. It was at Succoth, meaning "shelters," that Jacob stopped as a resting place to let his family and herds catch their breath.

Because he built "shelters" there for his cattle, that is why the place was named Succoth (v. 17).

Later Jacob would continue his journey as he would go for a while to Shechem (v. 18). There he purchased from the sons of Hamor, the father of Shechem, the plot of ground for "a hundred pieces of silver, where he then pitched his tent." There it was that he also erected an altar and named the altar "El Elohe Israel," meaning "mighty God of Israel" (v. 20). This portion of land is where the Israelites would also later bury the bones of Joseph (Joshua 24:32), and therefore it is a further promise of God's ultimate fulfillment of his promise-plan.

Summary: Some may still ask what it was that made Jacob seem undefeatable. When wrestling with God, it was not his hip but his faith that was most affected. It was by his faith that he received anew from the God of the promise-plan. It was because of Jacob's victorious faith that he inherited the blessing God had given to Abraham and Isaac. It is from Jacob's fight, with the wrestler he refused to let go of, that his name was changed from Jacob, meaning "deceiver," to "Israel," meaning "God fights" [for him]. His name, therefore, denotes a spiritual demeanor that is determined by faith, not that which is determined by flesh and blood or human prowess!

Conclusions

1. Jacob anticipated the worst in meeting his brother, but Esau took the initiative and ran to his long-lost brother and embraced and kissed him.

2. Jacob put a gift of droves of animals out in front of him to soften his brother's heart and the memory of his stealing the blessing and birthright from Esau.

3. Esau is impressed with the wives, family, and herds that Jacob had accumulated in the quarter of century he was away from his home.

4. Jacob arrived at the city of Shechem where Abraham had first received the promise of the land of Canaan (Gen. 12:6–7), where Jacob's well was located, and where later they would bury Joseph's bones.

Questions for Thought or Discussion

1. What do you think might have caused a change in Esau's heart over the years while Jacob was absent?

2. Why do you think that Jacob insisted that Esau should accept the droves of animals he had sent ahead of him? Was Jacob trying to quietly witness to the fact that God was faithful to his promise to him?

3. What do you gather from the fact that Esau offered twice to accompany Jacob and his entourage to their home?

4. Why do you think Jacob turned down such a kind offer?

5. Why do you think Jacob bought the piece of ground from the sons of Hamor and then set up an altar there?

Lesson 10

The Rape of Jacob's Daughter Dinah

Genesis 34:1–31

With all the dishonesty, savagery, and deceit it includes, chapter 34 is one of the most disturbing chapters in the Bible. Is it any wonder that the name of God appears nowhere in this chapter that is marked by such a mean story of rape, anger, deceit, greed, murder, violence, and selfishness? It certainly underscores its depravity. Instead of this passage focusing on the twelve men who were born in Jacob's household, this time we are told about his daughter Dinah, who was born to Leah (see Gen. 30:21).

Thus, when Jacob's family had left Paddan-Aram, they came to settle first in Succoth and then in Shechem, where Dinah suddenly becomes the center of attention in a conflict that arises between the patriarch Jacob and the Shechemites, local inhabitants of Canaan. Therefore, it raises the issue of conditions for an acceptable relationship with the host society and the need for spiritual moral and ethical separation between Jacob's family and the hosting Canaanites. This lesson will explore these issues.

The Local Son of a Hivite Prince Debases Jacob's Daughter Dinah by Raping Her – 34:1–4

The son of a prince in the land of Canaan was captivated by Jacob's daughter Dinah. He saw her when she decided one day to venture forth from her tent to visit the daughters of the land (v. 1). The son's name was "Shechem son of Hamor the Hivite," and "his heart was [so] drawn to Dinah" that when he saw her, "he took her and violated her" (vv. 2–3). Dinah would have been about fourteen at the time, when she was accosted by Shechem, for which her two brothers took revenge on her behalf. The brothers were not very old at the time; Simeon was 21 years old, and Levi was in his 20th year.

In a much-later case of rape in the Bible, one of King David's sons, Amnon, raped his half-sister Tamar (2 Sam. 7:13). As so often happens in situations like this, in the case of Amnon, his passionate desire turned to disgust after he raped Tamar. His passion quickly turned into hate for her, but this reversal of passion was not true in the case of Shechem, for after he had violated Dinah, "his heart was drawn to Dinah daughter of Jacob, and he loved the girl and spoke tenderly to her" (v. 3). Shechem was so love-struck over Dinah that he urged his father Hamor, "Get me this girl as my wife" (v. 4). In that time and culture, marriage was the business of parents, and it was arranged according to domestic protocol. Hamor was pleased with the idea, so he offered to bring as large a bridal price and gift as Jacob and his sons wanted (v. 12).

Jacob Holds His Peace on This Matter Until His Sons Return from the Field – 34:5–7

Jacob's immediate reaction to the news that his daughter had been raped by a Hivite ruler's son was to hold his peace until his sons returned from shepherding the sheep out in the fields (v. 5). But these brothers, after they had heard what had happened to their sister, were at once "filled with grief and fury, because Shechem had done a disgraceful thing in Israel by lying with [their sister]" (v. 7).

This passage began calmly, with Dinah going out of her tent to see the women of the land, yet by the time we have gone a little way into the text, two primary attitudes appear, *eros* and *eris*— "passion" and "strife." Up to this point, all the interactions between Jacob's family and the tribal society of the Canaanites here have been between the men, but now the women are involved. But this incident aborts any further attempt to mix or mingle the two groups. One moment Shechem is forcing his love on Dinah, and the next moment he's appealing to her by "speaking tenderly" (v. 3), which literally means he "spoke to [her] heart." Was he, by this change of language, attempting to assuage his own guilty conscience for what he had done and then expressing a desire to placate a sense of moral outrage he saw coming from Dinah's family? There is no question that Dinah's brothers were outraged at what Shechem had perpetrated against the honor of Dinah and her family.

Prince Hamor Urges Jacob's Sons to Form an Alliance with Them – 34:8–12

Shechem's father, Prince Hamor, tried to talk with Jacob about the marriage of his son Shechem to Jacob's daughter by indicating that his son was deeply in love with Dinah (v. 8). Hamor, by now, will agree to any amount for a bride-price that Jacob and his sons can name, but the only non-negotiable issue is that Shechem really wants to marry Dinah! Of course, the fact that Jacob and his sons could name any amount of money as a bride-price was extremely appealing, for this was their flesh and blood that was being so highly esteemed. Indeed, from that point of view, they had come a long way, baby! However, if Jacob and his family consented to any amount with Hamor, the family would be consenting to blending with a heathen family, and thus they would be forfeiting their redemptive calling. Moreover, had Dinah's brothers allowed the matter of the marriage to be settled by an amount of silver, they too would have defiled their own princely nobility and exchanged it all for mammon! This, Jacob, and his sons refused to do—which was a positive moral step. However, this move in the direction of moral righteousness was quickly ruined and reduced to evil, when two sons came up with a plan for revenge that involved murder. If the Lord had not providentially intervened, this might have proven to be the basis for the destruction of Jacob's family and the whole promise-plan of God.

The Sons of Jacob Deceitfully Argue That They Cannot Give Their Sister to an Uncircumcised Man – 34:13–18

Jacob's sons knew from the beginning that what they were suggesting, in what looked like good faith, was really part of a deceitful package that would bring death to all the men in this Hivite tribe (v. 13). The brothers argued that since Shechem was uncircumcised, as was the whole tribe of Hivites, they could not allow their sister to marry Shechem, for to do so would be a "disgrace" to them (v. 14).

Had Jacob's sons learned from their father a few dirty tricks from his moments of previous sins? Worst of all, Jacob's sons were about to use the holy ceremony of circumcision, which had been set up much earlier with Jacob's grandfather Abraham as a sign of the Abrahamic Covenant, as a principle of deceit. Herein was the height of desecration wherein the sacred was turned into a profane and murderous intent, for it would be how they would murder all the males of the city!

Shechem and Hamor were completely duped by the brothers' suggestion, one that appeared plausible and actionable enough. So, father and son went to the gateway of their city, where traditionally all formal business and legal matters were transacted, to make a proposal to all the male Shechemites. This included allowing themselves to be circumcised so Shechem could marry this Jewish girl named Dinah, and the same intermarriage possibilities would now also exist between the families in the future!

We could ask: Why would a stronger and more-established people like the Hivites be willing to adopt the ritual ceremony of a smaller group of newcomers? Perhaps Simeon and Levi, who appear to be the main architects of this ceremonial prerequisite for intermarriage between the two tribes, were making what they had hoped the Shechemites would see as an outrageous requirement—one that would blunt Shechem's ardor for Dinah, so Israel and the Hivites could just go their separate ways! But it is not clear that Simeon and Levi were thinking along these lines!

Hamor and Shechem Urge the Men of Their City to Consent to These Terms – 34:19–24

Shechem did not hesitate to fulfill the terms of the agreement (v. 19), for he was thoroughly consumed by his love for Dinah. Moreover, the rite of circumcision was not all that novel or foreign to the Hivites; the custom apparently was observed among some of the Canaanites and Egyptians. The princely pair returned to their city to proclaim the nature of the alliance that would make possible this arrangement between the two groups. To sweeten the deal for any Hivites who might be somewhat skeptical, the two men mentioned that the cattle of Jacob and sons, their beasts of burden, and their property in general could be looked upon as being their own (v. 23). This part of the alliance may have been a part of that treaty that Jacob and family did not hear, but it perhaps became a rhetorical device to help get any hesitant Shechemites to join the alliance. Accordingly, every male left the city gate agreeing to be circumcised (v. 24).

Dinah's Brothers, Simeon and Levi, Suddenly on the Third Day After Circumcision, Attack Every Hivite Male – 34:25–29

The Hivite male population were all circumcised, but weakened by the pain and loss of blood, they were in no shape to fight against Simeon and Levi. These two sons of Jacob, the ringleaders, were direct offspring of Leah, as was Dinah. After they massacred all the males in the city, they plundered the city of its wealth, taking as captives their women and children as well. The violence and savagery dished out by Simeon and Levi was horrific. The attackers took the city's sheep, oxen, and donkeys and made them their own. They fell on the people brutally and mercilessly.

Conclusion: Simeon and Levi Made Jacob's Name Stink Throughout the Land – 34:30–31

Jacob reproved both of his sons who had masterminded this whole operation, for he feared that now his rather small family, in comparison to the enclaves of Canaanites and Perizzites, would be subject to any number and all sorts of attacks from those who sympathetically heard what Jacob's family had done to the Shechemites. If any or all these natives in the land gathered against Jacob and his family, they would easily be able to hit them and destroy both Jacob and all his house, for they were still a comparatively small family group.

Jacob then decried what Simeon and Levi had done, but they both tried to justify what they had executed by saying, "Should he [Shechem] have treated our sister like a prostitute?" (v. 31)

Conclusions

1. We more than casually note that God's name occurs nowhere in Genesis 34. Do you think this was deliberate?

2. The city of Shechem gained its namesake from one of the sons of Hamor the Hivite, which may indicate he was already spoiled. This city played a major part in Yeshua's ministry to the Samaritan woman in John's gospel at Jacob's Well (John 4).

3. Shechem raped Jacob's daughter Dinah, and two of her brothers wanted to get revenge for such an act.

4. The loss of life and violence meted out by Simeon and Levi, Dinah's brothers, was terrible, indeed.

5. Jacob's deathbed blessing on Simeon and Levi would end up being a curse on both of them (Gen. 9:5–7), for their descendants would be scattered far and wide because of what they did.

Questions for Thought or Discussion

1. Do you think our Lord purposely omitted his name from this chapter because of its awful content? Why then was this chapter included in the Bible?

2. What do you think might have been Dinah's purpose in going into the city, as she and her family were newcomers to town?

3. Is there any evidence in this passage that Shechem's act of raping Dinah caused him internal guilt and an accusing conscience?

4. Why was the request that the Shechemite men be circumcised offensive to God and a form of secularizing what was a sacred act in Scripture?

5. How valid do you think Simeon and Levi's excuse was (v. 31)?

Lesson 11

Jacob Returns to Bethel

Genesis 35:1–29

It is impossible to say how much time elapsed between the events of Genesis 34, which recorded the rape of Dinah, and the events of Genesis 35. But it is clear that God instructed Jacob to leave Shechem and proceed south to Bethel. There he was told he was to build an altar to the Lord, the same Sovereign Lord who had appeared to him when he camped that night at Bethel and had the dream-vision of angels ascending and descending a ladder from heaven to earth! The elapsed time amounted to at least 20 years while Jacob stayed in Haran, serving 14 years to work off the bride-price for his two wives Leah and Rachel, plus another six years in pay he received for tending Laban's herds (Gen. 31:38–41). Let us look at this final text in the life of Jacob a little more closely.

The Return to Bethel and the Death of Rachel's Nurse, Deborah – 35:1–8

As Jacob returned from Paddan-Aram, he stopped to build the dwellings at Succoth, then went on to Shechem, and finally headed out for Bethel. Each stop brought him nearer to home and to his father, Isaac. Why he had stayed so long in Shechem is unknown, but now with Simeon and Levi's atrocious act, it was necessary they move on. The town the Lord directed him to go to was Bethel, the place where he had had the dream of the ladder that reached to heaven. In fact, Elohim had ordered him to go to Bethel to dwell and build an altar to God, who had appeared to him before. Jacob called

God the One "who answered me in the day of my distress and who has gone with me wherever I have gone" (v. 3).

However, before Jacob left Shechem, he ordered his whole household: "Get rid of the foreign gods you have with you and purify yourselves and change your clothes" (v. 2). Much of this pagan paraphernalia was jewelry, amulets, charms, and rings. Jacob buried all these idolatrous trinkets under a large tree near Shechem (v. 4). He knew such worship of foreign gods and the use of charms and amulets was going on in his family, for now that such vile acts as the brothers perpetrated had taken place among them, it was time they as a family no longer tolerated such evil actions nor idolatry. Perhaps Jacob had been too indulgent toward his wives, especially because of his affection for Rachel, who seemed to have pilfered the household gods (31:19) of Laban. Jacob wanted his family to be purified and cleansed of all their sin as they set forth in the land God had promised to give them.

Then the family came to Bethel to dwell, where Jacob recalled the vow he had made to God as he was on his outbound journey away from his home and the land of Canaan (28:22). As always, God was with Jacob, as he had promised (e.g., 28:15). Accordingly, when Jacob arrived at Bethel, he built the altar God had commanded him to build. This altar was now the fifth altar that had been erected in patriarchal history. These five altars were:

1. Abraham erected one near Bethel – 12:8
2. Abraham erected another altar in Mamre near Hebron – 12:8
3. Isaac erected one in Beersheba – 26:25
4. Jacob erected an altar in Shechem – 33:20
5. Jacob erected another in Bethel – 35:6

These altars may merely be places for devotion to the Lord, for nowhere does Scripture say that sacrifice was offered on them. Jacob did give his reason for building an altar at Bethel: "because it was there that God had revealed himself to him when he was fleeing from his brother" (v. 7b).

Just about this time, Deborah, Rebekah's nurse, passed away (v. 8). Deborah had accompanied Rebekah all the way from their homestead in Haran (24:59). What's more, she may have outlived Rebekah, the one she served all her life. The last note we have about Rebekah is in Genesis 29:12. Deborah had died after a long life of service and was buried under an oak tree near Bethel. Because this was the spot where the mourning and weeping for her death took place, the place was named Allon Bacuth, meaning "oak of weeping/mourning" (v. 8).

The Renewing of the Honor Attached to the Name of Israel – 35:9–15

For a second time, Jacob's name was changed to "Israel" (vv. 9–10; see 32:28). But why should this naming process take place a second time? Was there some attempt to remove the negative aspect of this name, that Jacob "struggled with God" (32:28)? It is true, of course, that Jacob, by now at least, is not the same man we saw earlier in his life. Was the Lord now restoring honor to Jacob's new name "Israel"?

Previously, God had revealed himself as "God Almighty" when he promised Abraham that he would be the father of many descendants (17:1–8), but now he revealed himself to Jacob with the same promise (vv. 11–12). The Lord's words are most important, for first of all, the words "be fruitful and increase in number" (v. 11) are reminiscent of God's primeval blessing at the time of creation

(Gen. 1:28). God was still active in his ancient promise to bless all humanity. But most importantly, God promised the "land" would be given to Abraham (Gen. 12:7), but it was now further conferred to Jacob (v. 12).

Out of gratitude for God's sustaining his promises about a "seed," "the land," and now "kings," Jacob set up a pillar and consecrated it by pouring oil on it at the very spot where he had named the site Bethel, meaning "House of God" (vv. 14–15; see 28:18–19).

The Birth of Benjamin and the Death of Rachel – 35:16–20

At this point, Jacob and his family left Bethel and journeyed south just as Rachel was in her last stages of pregnancy. As they traveled, Rachel began to have severe labor pains, but her midwife tried to cheer her up by assuring her that she was having another son (v. 17). However, sad as it may seem, Rachel died as a result of childbirth (v. 18).

Just before Rachel passed away, she named her newborn son Ben-Oni, "son of my trouble," but Jacob renamed the boy Benjamin, meaning "son of my right hand" or "son of the south." This possible dual meaning is because the ancient Hebrews always faced east, meaning the southern direction was always to the right.

The writer took pains to remark that the place where Rachel was buried was Ephrath, which was the older name for Bethlehem (see 1 Sam. 17:12; Micah 5:2). Moreover, once again, Jacob set up over Rachel's tomb a "pillar" to mark the spot of her grave (v. 20). Of the three patriarchs Abraham, Isaac, and Jacob, Rachel is the only wife who is not buried in the cave of Machpelah in Hebron alongside her husband! Instead, she was buried alongside the road leading to

Ephrath. To this day, there is a tomb near Bethlehem called "Rachel's tomb," but whether that identification is correct is unclear.

Reuben's Act of Dishonoring His Father's Concubine Bilhah – 35:21–22a

Jacob, a man who was always on the move, moved on once more and finally pitched his tent at Migdal Eder. It was at this spot that Jacob's oldest son Reuben fell from his father's favor and from his position as the firstborn in the family, for Reuben went into the tent and lay with his father's concubine Bilhah (v. 22). Nothing further is said at this time about what Reuben did than the fact that Jacob "heard of it." Reuben lost this prominent place in the birth order of Jacob's sons because of this sin (Gen. 49:3–4; 1 Chronicles 5:1). But it is interesting to note that Jacob is called "Israel" three times in vv. 21–22a.

The List of Jacob's Sons by Their Mother's Names – 35:22b–26

The birth of Benjamin as Jacob's twelfth son makes the roster of his family now complete. Leah's six sons are listed first, being Reuben, Simeon, Levi, Judah, Issachar, and Zebulun, followed by Rachel's two sons, Joseph and Benjamin. Then the two sons of Rachel's handmaid Bilhah follow: Dan and Naphtali, with the two sons born to Leah's handmaid Zilpah: Gad and Asher. These were the total number of Jacob's sons.

Jacob Arrives Home; His Father Isaac Dies – 35:27–29

Jacob returned to be with his father Isaac in Mamre, near Kiriath Arba (an older name for Hebron), a place where Abraham and Isaac had often chosen to live. Isaac died at the age of 180, which exceeded his father Abraham's longevity by five years.

It is of very special note that when Isaac breathed his last and was "gathered to his people," his two sons Esau and Jacob were there. Apparently, the reconciliation between the two men really was holding and so there is a blessed note on which the story of Jacob is finished.

It is true that after Isaac died, Jacob lived another twenty-seven years, for he was 120 years old at the time of his father's death (see vv. 25:26, 47:28), but nothing more was added to the story of his involvement in the promise-plan of God. But the patriarchal era was rapidly coming to a close, and the attention would now shift in the biblical story from these three old-time worthies to a younger generation that will emerge from 400 years of bondage in Egypt—from Joseph becoming Pharaoh's regent to the Exodus under Moses.

Conclusions

1. God called Jacob to leave Shechem and to go to Bethel, where he was to build an altar to the Lord his God.
2. Before Jacob left Shechem, after the massacre of all the males in the Shechemite tribe, Jacob called for a time of spiritual and moral cleansing and revival by burying all the idols, charms and ear rings devoted to the false gods and idols that were among his family and household.
3. God promised Jacob he would multiply and increase his descendants, give him the land of Canaan to live in, and raise up kings among his descendants.
4. Rachel died as Jacob and his entourage approached Bethlehem, and there she was buried outside Ephrath, where a pillar was erected that became a marker for her grave.
5. Isaac died after living 180 years and was buried by his two sons Esau and Jacob.

Questions for Thought or Discussion

1. Why did God twice rename Jacob "Israel"? Can you suggest any reasons for this action? Did this mean his struggle with God and men was over?
2. Why do you think Jacob was moved to initiate a revival at Shechem before he and his family left? How important is it to be cleansed and purified by God and his word if we are going to face a new chapter in our lives?
3. How did God protect Jacob and his family after the atrocity committed by Simeon and Levi? Was Jacob afraid? Wherein did he find comfort and help?
4. Why was Reuben dismissed from his role and right as holder of the birthright in the family? To whom did this honor pass?
5. What evidence do you see of any moral or spiritual development in Jacob's life as he grew older?

Lesson 12

The Final Blessing and Death of Jacob

Genesis 49:1–50:14

The time for Jacob's departure had drawn near, so he summoned his favorite son Joseph to his side, for he intended to gather all his sons and to bless them all. Jacob had already blessed Pharaoh (Gen. 47:7–10) as well as Joseph's two sons Ephraim and Manasseh (48:20), but it was now time to bless his own sons as well. So, Joseph took the lead in "assembling" all Jacob's sons around him so they could hear what Jacob would tell them about their future (v. 2).

The Blessing of Jacob

This gathering was, as Jacob put it, "so I can tell you what will happen in the last days" (v. 1b). This expression "in the last days" only appears three times in the *Torah* (i.e., *Pentateuch*: here, 'The Blessing of Jacob' (vv. 1–28); 'The Burdens of Balaam' (Num. 24:14–24); and 'The Last Words of Moses' (Deut. 31:29). In all three of these prophetic poems, the expression "in the last days" refers to a coming future deliverance of Abraham's seed in the time around the Second Coming of the Lord. At the center of all three of these prophetic poems is a word about a coming king (Gen. 49:10; Num. 24:7; Deut. 33:5) who is connected to the house of Judah and the coming Messiah, namely Yeshua.

Jacob's words of blessing are commented on more in detail in my character study of Joseph, but one blessing in that group is so important and so significant that it helps us to see the picture of the future that Jacob held as he prepared for his death. It is the blessing that Jacob gave about Judah, his fourth son, borne by Leah (see vv. 49:8–12).

Ordinarily one would think Jacob's oldest son Reuben would have been honored with the blessing of the firstborn son, but he forfeited that honor when he slept with his father's handmaid. Likewise, recall Jacob's sons Levi and Simeon, in their outrageous assault on the Shechemites, because their prince had raped Dinah. These two sons of Jacob attacked the tribe of Shechem for this crime after promising that all would be well if they would be circumcised as they were. But while the men of Shechem were recovering from their circumcisions, Levi and Simeon slew all of them. Thus, the right of the firstborn was passed over both of them on to Joseph (Gen. 48:5). However, Psalm 78:67 makes it plain that Judah was not told that he was given the birthright either; instead, he was given the role of dominance as the "strongest" over his brothers and thus was the heir to the throne. As the psalmist put it:

> Then [the LORD] rejected the tents of Joseph; he did not choose the tribe of Ephraim, but he chose the tribe of Judah, Mount Zion, which he loved.

The Prophecy About Judah

Jacob's prophecies about Judah are so important that we want to connect them with this final study of Jacob. Jacob's words to Judah were more transparent than most of the images used for most of the blessing of the other brothers. To be sure, Judah is pictured as a "young lion" sleeping in his den after taking his prey there (v. 9), but v. 10 completes this picture, depicting Judah as a warrior, or a king who holds the scepter and ruler's staff, thereby announcing that Judah will hold the royal status and dominion "until he to whom it belongs shall come" (v. 10b). A number of the English translations (e.g., KJV) left untranslated the Hebrew word *Shiloh* in this passage, but it means "the one to whom it belongs," as written out in full in Ezekiel 21:27b.

Even the Dead Sea Scroll 4Q "Patriarchal Blessing" was not in doubt as to what Genesis 49:10 meant, for it interpreted this passage in Genesis thus:

> "A ruler shall [not] depart from the tribe of Judah when Israel has dominion. [And] the one who sits on the throne of David [shall never] be cut off … until the Righteous Messiah, the Branch of David [from the tribe of Judah] has come…"

Just as amazing is the fact that this one who will come in the line of David will receive "the obedience of the nations" (v. 10b). It is important to note Jacob used in his blessing of Judah the plural "nations," indicating this kingship would extend far beyond the borders of Israel; it would see that it included "a community of peoples" (Gen. 28:3, 48:4). This same teaching appears in Psalm 2:8, where God "will make the nations your [Israel's] inheritance." Likewise, Daniel 7:13–14 agreed, for to the Son of Man "was given authority, glory, sovereign power, all peoples, nations and men of every language [to] worship him."

Genesis 49:11–12 includes, furthermore, images of prosperity and abundance. Thus, the donkey would be tethered to the choicest vines while the clothes in that coming day would be washed in vintage grape juice. This means that the produce of the fields would be so plentiful that it would not matter if beasts of burden were hitched to these choice vines that might be ripped away if the animal suddenly took off from where it was hitched. Moreover, the produce of the fields would be so abundant that grape juice could be used in place of water to wash their clothes! Verse 12 draws a picture of the well-being of the king of Judah so that his eyes were darker than wine and his teeth were whiter than milk. This too was a picture of opulence and wealth, for the picture of that future was most bright and promising.

The Funeral Entourage

When Jacob had finished blessing all twelve of his sons, his day for departure had come. Jacob had announced that his son Joseph would be the one who would close his eyes when he died (v. 46:4). This was an honor reserved for the person who was closest to the deceased. Joseph "was truly heartbroken over his father's death, for he "threw himself on his father and wept over him and kissed him" (50:1).

Joseph then gave the order for his father to be embalmed in the manner of the Egyptian culture. The scriptural text spent over one-half of the final chapter in Genesis describing all that went into mourning for his father Jacob. It took "forty days" for the Egyptians to wrap Jacob's mummy and preserve some of his body parts in a similar way (50:3). This was followed by another period of mourning for thirty days, making a total of seventy days for the total time of Jacob's funeral (50:3b). It is not clear whether Pharaoh involved the whole nation of Egypt over this two-and-a-half-month period, but it is certain that this Jewish foreigner had kept Egypt and the nations of that whole part of the world from starving and being dissolved.

Jacob, of course, had given careful instructions to make sure his body was taken back to Canaan, for he did not want to be buried in Egypt. Instead, he wanted to be buried in the same place where his grandfather Abraham was entombed and where his father Isaac was also buried (49:29–32, 50:5). Pharaoh granted the request Jacob had made of his son to be buried in Canaan (v. 50:4) and saw to it that Joseph's father's funeral was much like that of an official dignitary, for Jacob's son had occupied the number-two spot in the chain of command in Egypt for a good period of time.

Pharaoh equipped Joseph and the funeral party with "chariots and horsemen," thus the funeral cortege ended up being "a very large [and an impressive] company" (v. 50:9). They must have been an impressive sight as they marched along in line towards Canaan; in fact, it did attract the attention of the local Canaanite population (v. 11).

There were three different groups that were part of this funeral procession: those who were part of Pharaoh's administration (v. 7), the males who were part of Jacob's family (v. 8), and a military escort that rode along in the chariots with the horsemen (v. 9).

The funeral march continued until they came to Goren ha-Atad ("the threshing floor of Atad"), where they paused for seven days as a time to raise an additional lament. To date we have not been able to identify the location of this site, but it is said to be "in the region of the Jordan" or "beyond the Jordan," which would put it in Transjordania on the east side of the Jordan River. Why the funeral cortege went over there is unknown. However, they must have returned around the south end of the Dead Sea as they eventually came to Hebron, where the relatives Jacob wanted to be buried with were located. The days of Jacob had come to an end, and he was with his Lord.

The Lives and Ministries of ELIJAH and ELISHA
His Names Are Wonderful
Barbara D. Malda
Come and Worship
Under THE FIG TREE
PATRICK GABRIEL LUMBROSO
Under THE VINE
PATRICK GABRIEL LUMBROSO
Making Eye Contact with God
You Bring the Bagels I'll Bring the Gospel
RUBIN
THE WORLD TO COME
Psalms & Proverbs
David H. Stern
MESSIANIC JUDAISM
STERN
GOD'S APPOINTED CUSTOMS
KASDAN
GOD'S APPOINTED TIMES
KASDAN
GATEWAYS TO TORAH
RABBI RUSSELL RESNIK
CREATION TO COMPLETION
RESNIK
Is Christ Really The End of The Law?
To the Ends of the Earth
On The Way to Emmaus
Dr. Jacques Doukhan
YESHUA
JEWISH NEW TESTAMENT COMMENTARY
MATTHEW PRESENTS YESHUA, KING MESSIAH
KASDAN
PHILIPPIANS

Printed in the United States
by Baker & Taylor Publisher Services